Charles Rogers

Memorials of the Scottish Families of Strachan and Wise

Charles Rogers

Memorials of the Scottish Families of Strachan and Wise

ISBN/EAN: 9783337243869

Printed in Europe, USA, Canada, Australia, Japan

Cover: Foto ©ninafisch / pixelio.de

More available books at **www.hansebooks.com**

MEMORIALS

OF THE

SCOTTISH FAMILIES

OF

STRACHAN AND WISE

BY THE

REV. CHARLES ROGERS, LL.D.

FELLOW OF THE SOCIETY OF ANTIQUARIES OF SCOTLAND; FELLOW OF THE ROYAL
HISTORICAL SOCIETY; MEMBER OF THE HISTORICAL SOCIETY OF QUEBEC;
AND CORRESPONDING MEMBER OF THE HISTORICAL AND
GENEALOGICAL SOCIETY OF NEW ENGLAND

EDINBURGH:
PRINTED BY M'FARLANE AND ERSKINE
(*late Schenck & M'Farlane*),
ST JAMES SQUARE.

PREFACE.

OF these *Memorials* a first edition was, in 1873, printed for private circulation. In matters of detail the present edition is more ample, while it is free from certain errors which crept into the former issue. Two genealogical narratives, discovered subsequent to the printing of the text, are deemed sufficiently important to find a place in the Appendix. The entire Memoir has been framed on authentic materials, which are systematically quoted or referred to.

GRAMPIAN LODGE, FOREST HILL, SURREY,
December 1876.

MEMORIALS

OF THE

FAMILIES OF STRACHAN AND WISE.

THE *strath* or valley, through which the river *Aan* conveys its waters from Mount Battack to the river Feugh, on the western borders of Kincardineshire, has given name to the surrounding territory. The district now termed *Strachan*, was formerly known as Strathechyn, Strathethyne, or Strathawchin. A charter, dated about the year 1215, sets forth that Waldeve or Waltheof de Strathecan granted the lands of Blackerock to the monks of St Andrews. These lands were bounded by the streams Feugh and Dye, in the district of Strachan. In the same charter Ranulp or Randolph is mentioned as son and apparent heir of Waldeve or Waltheof of Strathecan (Regist. Priorat. Sti. Andreæ).

About 1220 a charter is witnessed by Waldeve de Strachachyn; and in 1278 John de Strachachyn, son and heir of the late John of Strachachyn, resigned his lands of Beth[1] Waldeve into the hands of

[1] The lands of Beth or Beath form a parish of that name, about seven miles to the east of Dunfermline.

Alexander II., when the king conveyed them to the Abbey of Dunfermline (Registrum de Dunfermlyn). At this period the territory of Strachan was conveyed by marriage to Sir Alexander Frazer, Thane of Cowie, chamberlain to King Robert the Bruce. In 1316 Sir Alexander received a royal charter "de omnibus et singulis terris de Strachethyne de Essuly et Achencrooks, faciendo nobis et heredibus nostris dictus Alexander et heredes sui, forinsecum servitium, quantum pertinet ad predictam baroniam." In the lands of Strachan, Sir Alexander Frazer was succeeded by his son John, who was knighted. Margaret, only daughter of Sir John, married Sir William Keith, Marischal of Scotland. In 1376, Robert II. confirmed to Robert de Keth the barony and forests of Strathachyn, on the resignation of his parents, William de Keth, Marischal, and Margaret Frazer. Among the papers of the Countess of Rothes, at Leslie House, Fifeshire, is preserved a charter under the Great Seal, by King Robert III., confirming a charter, which is therein engrossed, by Alexander de Leslie, Earl of Ross, to his cousin, Sir George de Leslie, Lord of Rothes, for his good and faithful counsel and service, of all his lands of Woodfield, Frisky of Esly, Balmain, and Strachan, in the barony of Kincardine, and the yearly annual rents out of the said lands of Kincardine; and for which lands and others, Sir George paid to the Earl of Ross in his great need 200 merks Scots, to satisfy the king for the relief, as well of the earldom of Ross, as of his other lands; to be held of the said earl and his lawful heirs; whom failing, of the king, in fee and heritage for ever, giving therefore yearly three suits to three head courts, to be held at Kincardine. This charter contains a clause of absolute warrandice, and is dated at Perth the 27th of February 1400; the witnesses thereto being—Robert Stuart, Duke of Albany, Earl of Fife and Monteith; Murdoch Stuart, his son and heir, Justiciar on the north side of Forth, Lord of Kincleivin; David

Lindesay, Earl of Crawford, William de Lindsay, Lord Byers, and others. The charter of confirmation is dated at Scoon, the 4th of March 1400, and the witnesses thereto are—Walter, Bishop of St Andrews; Gilbert, Bishop of Aberdeen, Chancellor to the King; David, Duke of Rothesay, Earl of Carrick and Athole, and Steward of Scotland; Robert, Duke of Albany; Archibald, Earl of Douglas, Lord of Galloway; and James of Douglas, Lord of Dalkeith, and Thomas de Erskine, Knights (Report of Historical Commission, part iv., p. 494).

While the lands of Strachan fell into the possession of the female branch, the representation of the family in the male line was continued. In a decree at the instance of William of Strinelyne, laird of Cadon, dated 21st January 1442, and pronounced by James, Bishop of St Andrews, and others, respecting certain lands in Dumbartonshire, is named among the assessors of the Court, "Alexander of Strathachyn, procuratore for the lorde of Kethe." On the 13th April 1452, he received from James II. a charter of half the lands of Keir, Perthshire (Stirling of Keir Family Papers, pp. 217, 227).

During the reign of David II. (1328-1370) a charter was granted by Thomas, Earl of Mar, to Adam Strachan and his wife Margaret, the earl's cousin, and to their issue, of the lands of Glenkenety, now Glenkindy,[1] in the parish of Strathdon, Aberdeenshire. This charter was in the possession of Sir Alexander Strachan of Glenkindy, and Nisbet remarks he had seen it (Nisbet's Heraldry, vol. i., p. 326). William Strathachin, described as "vicarius perpetuus Beatæ Mariæ ad nives," was in 1499, Rector of the University of King's College, Aberdeen. Gilbert Strathauchyn, evidently of the same family, was rector in 1531 (Sinclair's Statistical Account, vol. xxi.). On the 20th July 1510,

[1] An old English ballad has been adapted to the Scottish meridian under the name of Glenkindie (Roberts' Legendary Ballads, p. 26).

William Strachan, son and apparent heir of Duncan Strachan of Glenkindy, received a precept for a charter of the lands of Glenkindy, reserving the liferent thereof to the said Duncan and a reasonable terce to Margaret Lundy, his spouse (Reg. Sec. Sig., vol. iv.). On the 7th February 1528, William Strachan of Glenkindy received a remission for his absence from the army at the battle of Solway (Privy Seal Gifts, vol. ix.). A royal letter, dated 25th April 1545, was addressed to Sir George Strathauchin, granting him and "his heirs and assignys, a gift of all the goods, movable and immovable, pertaining to Alexander Law, by reason of his escheat for absenting himself from the army ordained to be convened at Ancrum" (Reg. Sec. Sig., vol. xix., fol. 7b). In the "Chronicle of Aberdeen" occurs the following entry: "Wilyem Strayquhen, sone to the Lard Glenkindy, departtit the xi. day of November, the yeir of God 1575 yeris" (Miscellany of the Spalding Club).

On the 3d June 1630, the Privy Council received at Holyrood a submission between Alexander Fraser of Philorth and Alexander Strachan of Glenkindy anent the satisfaction to be given by the latter to the former for "the insolence committed be him agains the said laird of Philorth upon the Hie Street of Edinburgh, a litle above the mercat croce thairof, in the month of March last, by the persute and invasioun of him for his bodilie harm, and slaughter and hurting and wounding him to the effusion of his blood in great quantitie." The judges appointed by the council were James, Lord Ogilvie of Airlie; Sir Alexander Gordon of Cluny, Knight Baronet; Andrew Fraser of Muckalls; William Forbes of Tolquhore; and Thomas Fraser of Streachin (Reg. Sec. Sig., vol. 1630-32, fol. 232).

In a bond dated at Aberdeen 22d January 1653, are named Alexander Strachan, elder, and Alexander Strachan, younger, of Glenkindie (Reg. of Deeds, vol. 591). In the "Minute-Book of Confirmed Testaments of the

Commissariat of Aberdeen" is named, on the 7th October 1731, Sir Patrick Strachan of Glenkindie; and in the same record, on the 7th July 1732, Alexander Strachan, his brother-german.[1]

By a member of the House of Strachan of Glenkindie were acquired the lands of Kinaldie, Aberdeenshire. On the 17th July 1627, Patrick Strachan of Kynnadie obtained a remission "for any hurt he had caused to John Fraser in Elrick in revenge for the said John and his servant, John Fordice, and their accomplices having attacked the said Patrick on a Sabbath day while he was at public worship, in May 1625, by coming behind him with huge cudgels, striking him on the head therewith, and wounding him on various parts of the body to the effusion of blood, and would have deprived him of life but for the interference of the people then assembled" (Paper Reg. of the Great Seal, vol. ii., fol. 299).

On the 13th August 1651, Patrick Strachan "of Kynnadie" granted a discharge to Alexander Urquhart of Dunlagis for 300 merks; Alexander Strachan, younger of Glenkindie, is one of the witnesses (Reg. of Deeds, vol. 578, fol. 21).

On the 16th December 1534, William Strachan of Tibbertie and Janet Auchinleck, his spouse, obtained gift of the ward of the lands of Blackhall, in the regality of Garearch and shire of Aberdeen, formerly belonging to William Blackhall of that ilk, and Janet Strachan, his spouse, both deceased (Reg. Sec. Sig., vol. xxvii., fol. 90). On the 14th February 1539, George Strathachin of Easter Lesmurdie, and Margaret Gordon, his wife, received confirmation of a charter of the lands of Balcherge, Banffshire (Reg. Mag. Sig., lib. xxvi., No. 305). James Strathauchin of Lesmordy, and Elizabeth Abercrombie his spouse, received on

---

[1] In the Charter Room of the Earl of Fife, at Duff House, are preserved title-deeds, etc., illustrative of the descent of several illustrious families, including the Strachans of Glenkindie (Hist. Com. Report, part iv., p. 516).

1st November 1549, precept for a charter of lands of Thombayne and Lesmordy (Reg. Sec. Sig., vol. xxiii., fol. 57b). On the 31st July 1572, Andrew Strachan of Tullyfrusky obtained gift of the ward and non-entry of the lands belonging to the late James Strachan of Lesmurdie, with the marriage of Patrick Strachan, son and apparent heir of the said James (Reg. Sec. Sig., vol. xi., fol. 117). At Banff, on the 26th August 1601, Arthur Strachan, in Innerithnie, only brother and apparent heir of the late Captain John Strachan, and on behalf of Margaret and Marion, his sisters, and their husbands, made renunciation in favour of Alexander Pearson and John Young, merchant-burgesses of Edinburgh, for money paid by them, of all right the granter and his sisters had to the guidis, geir, jewellis, gold, silver, cunzeit and uncunzeit, horses, armour, apparell, and abulzementis of the said umquhill Captain John Strachan his body (Reg. of Deeds, vol. 80).

A scion of the House of Glenkindie obtained the lands of Culloden. On the 31st August 1639, a charter of the lands of Easter Culloden was granted to George Strachan, junior, on the resignation of his father, Alexander Strathauchin (Reg. Mag. Sig., lib. xxvi, No. 305; Reg. Sec. Sig., vol. xiii., fol. 26). George Strathauchin, son of Alexander Strathauchin, obtained a charter of the lands of Wester Culloden on the 16th December 1540 (Reg. Mag. Sig., lib. xxvii., No. 91).

From the northern counties of Aberdeen and Banff the House of Strachan migrated southward. According to Playfair, they acquired their first settlement in Kincardineshire through the marriage of Sir James Strathecan, or Strachan, with Agneta, heiress of Thornton. Playfair relates that among the family papers of Lord Saltoun was formerly preserved a charter granted by David II. in 1363 to Sir James Strathecan and his wife Agneta (Playfair's Baronetage, vol. iii., p. 167). In 1309, Valens de Thorntoun obtained from King Robert the Bruce a charter of lands in Kincardineshire bearing his name (Robertson's Index, i. 13). If the narrative of Playfair is correct, a daughter of Valens de Thornton may have carried the estate into the family of Strachan. It may here be remarked that the families of Strachan and of Thornton of that ilk frequently intermarried. On the 23d July 1557, John Thornton of that ilk, with consent of John Strachan of Claypottis and others, curators of the said John, obtained precept for confirmation of a charter in favour of Isabella Strachan, eldest daughter of Thomas Strachan of Carmylie, of the fourth part of Thornton in liferent in implement of the marriage-contract between the said John and Isabella (Reg. Sec. Sig., vol. xxviii., fol. 83). In April 1655, died, in the parish of Forgan, Fifeshire, "Euphame Strachan, Lady Thorntoun" (Com. Reg. of St Andrews, vol. xi.).

In a charter by David II. confirming to Walter Pitcarne the lands of Moneyethyn, and dated 15th December 1368, Duncan de Strathachyn is named as one of the witnesses (Fraser's Earls of Southesk, p. 489).

From David II., in 1365, Alexander Strathechin received a charter of the lands of Morphie Wester in Kincardineshire (Robertson's Index, 34, 10; Playfair's Baronetage, iii., clxvii.). Alexander de Strachan married Christian de Maule, only daughter of Sir Henry de Maule of Panmure, and received with her as dowry the lands of Carmyllie and Drummadith (Registrum de Panmure, vol. i., p. ccxi.). From David II. he obtained a royal charter confirming a charter by Henry Maule of Panmure, whereby he received the lands of Carmyle, Drummayeth, Hackmaugerum, Achyclare, and Moncur. He was by David II. appointed coroner of the counties of Forfar and Kincardine (Robertson's Index, 37, 6; 51, 37).

Of the marriage of Alexander de Strachan and his wife Christian de Maule, were born two sons, Alexander and Henry. To Henry of

8   *Memorials of the Families of Strachan and Wise.*

Strathekyn, younger son of Alexander Strachan, and to Ysoca his wife, Walter de Maule, lord of Panmure, his uncle, granted, on the 21st Septenrber 1346, a charter of three parts of the lands of Moncur in the barony of Panmure. The charter proceeds thus:

"To all who may see or hear this charter, I, Walter Maule, lord of Panmure, send greeting. Know ye that I have given, granted, and, by this present charter, have confirmed to Henry of Strathekyn, son of Christian, my sister, to Isocia de Strathekyn, wife of the said Henry, and to the heirs who may be begotten of them, three parts of the lands of Moncur, within the barony of Panmure, which I hold in chief from our lord the king: to be held by the same Henry, Isocia, and their descendants, from me and my heirs in feu and inheritance, in all divisions and appanages, such as meadows, pastures, fens, and marshes, free multure, and other privileges, conveniences, and rights pertaining to the said three parts, etc., on condition of doing out-door service to our lord the king, in as far as concerns the foresaid three parts of the lands; and of paying me and my heirs one shilling nominally of '*alba firma*'[1] at the Feast of Pentecost, at my castle of Panmure, if it be demanded, in place of all other service, custom, due, or similar tribute. Accordingly I, Walter, and my heirs, do make over, and for ever resign the said three parts, with their appurtenances, to the same Henry, Isocia, and heirs of the same as aforesaid, and guarantee them against all, male and female. In witness whereof I have placed my seal to these presents, at Moncur, on the 21st day of September, the year of our Lord 1346" (Regist. de Panmure, vol ii., p. 166).

Alexander Strachan, elder son of Alexander Strachan and Christian de Maule, succeeded his parents in the lands of Carmyllie. From William de Maule of Panmure he received, in 1361, a lease of the lands of Skryne, which had been possessed in wadset by Sir Robert Lauder, Knight. This instrument, translated from the Latin, proceeds thus:

"This is to certify, that, when the lands of Skryne, in the barony of Panmure, in Angus, had been mortgaged by the late Walter of Maule, lord of Panmure, to Sir Robert Lauder, knight, till the sum of one hundred and sixteen pounds four shillings sterling should be fully paid at a certain date by the said Walter, or his heirs, to the said Sir Robert: and seeing that Alexander of Strachechyn, lord of Karmylie, assisted William of Maule, son and heir of the late Walter, both by loans, and also by the greatest possible advice and aid of friends,

---

[1] Money paid by a vassal to his lord in lieu of the right possessed by the latter to lodge himself and retinue in his vassal's dwelling. Latterly it was used to signify a payment of one penny or other nominal duty.

to the redemption of said mortgage; and seeing that the business was effectively carried out by means of loans granted by Alexander for the use of William, for the getting back freely and fully the lands of Skryne as part of the property and demesne of Walter, out of the hands of Sir Robert,—the same William, now lord of Panmure, in acknowledgment of the friendship of Alexander, nor willing that ingratitude be laid to his charge, has assigned and granted in fee, for himself and heirs, to the said Alexander and his heirs, the whole of his lands of Skryne aforesaid, with their appanages, from the Feast of St Martin in winter 1361 to the end of five years after the Feast of Pentecost, next following after, to be had and held by the said Alexander, his heirs and assignees, to the end of the said five years, with all conveniences and liberties, privileges, dignities and forfeitures, and all other appurtenances concerning the said lands, or in any way likely to concern them. And the aforesaid Alexander, for the fee of the said lands and their appanages, shall pay, in name of the said William to the said Sir Robert, or his heirs or assignees, twenty merks sterling proportionably, on the Feast of St Martin aforesaid, and the Feast of Pentecost next to follow hereafter; and also to the said Sir Robert, six merks sterling yearly during the said five years, beginning to pay the said six merks at the said term of Pentecost. And the said lands of Skryne, with their appanages, shall remain freely in the hands of the said Alexander, for the two first years from the said Feast of Pentecost, without any payment being made to the said William in consideration of the said twenty merks paid to the said knight. If, however, the said knight should happen to die within the said two years, the said William shall not exact from the said Alexander aught of the said six merks, which the said Alexander, as aforesaid, should be bound to pay to the knight if living. Also in the last three of the five years aforesaid, the said Alexander shall pay ten merks yearly to the same William, and six merks to the said knight, if he be still alive, at the completion of the term. But if the said knight should be dead, let a full payment of the said sixteen merks be made by the said Alexander or his heirs, to the said William, at the completion of the period: also the said Alexander shall, at the completion of the oft-quoted term of five years, restore the lands of Skryne in good order and well peopled. To the faithful observance of all and each of these their articles, the said William and Alexander have solemnly and truly sworn in turn on the holy Gospels, pledging their faith by hand. And their seals are mutually appended to the parts of the bond now and henceforward remaining, and to each part likewise the seal of the aforesaid knight is appended. At Arbroath the 29th day of October 1361" (Regist. de Panmure, vol. ii., pp. 174, 175).

From John of Glasleter, of that ilk, Alexander Strachan of Carmyllie received, in 1365, a disposition of his lands of Awchinlar. The disposition, which is granted with the consent of William of Maule, his lord superior, proceeds thus:

"To all, etc., I, John Glasleter of that ilk, etc. Know ye that I have granted, and with the consent and free will of William of Maule, my lord superior, for myself and heirs for ever, have confirmed to Alexander de Strathekyne, lord of Carnyllie, his heirs and assignees, the whole of my lands of Awchinlar—viz., the half thereof, with appanages, situated, together with the half of the pasture land and Quythyle, below the territory of said village, in return for a certain sum of money which the said Alexander put into my own hands and paid over in my great necessity, the same to be held by the said Alexander, his heirs and assignees, in perpetual fee and heirship, throughout all its just and ancient limits, freely, peacefully, well, and without dispute, with marshes, fens, turbaries, rushy-meadows, shrubberies, roads, pathways, streams, pools, wells, and multures, with free entrance and exit, and all other conveniences, freedoms, and privileges below as above ground, specified or not specified, pertaining to the said lands, or which may at any time in future come to pertain to them. Which lands, with appanages aforesaid, I, the said John, and my heirs, do to the said Alexander and his heirs and assignees in all respects as above mentioned, guarantee, make over, and for ever resign. In witness whereof my seal is appended to this my present charter at Arbroath, at the Feast of the Purification of the Blessed Virgin, A.D. 1365, in presence of the following witnesses: a reverend father in Christ, Sir William, abbot of Arbroath; Alexander Skrymgeour, Galfred Kuych, William Scrymgeour, John Makpesse, Galfred de Dalgernok, Sir Michael de Manwel, monk of the same monastery, and many others" (Regist. de Panmure, vol. ii., pp. 176, 177).

By a charter, dated at Perth 5th February 1382, Robert II. confirmed the charters granted to Alexander Strachan of Carmyllie and his wife Christian, by Sir Henry de Maule and John of Glasleter, of the lands of Carmyllie, Awchinlar, and others. Of this instrument a translation follows:

"Robert, by the grace of God, King of Scots, to all honest men throughout his realm, clerical and lay, greeting. *Know ye*, that we have approved, ratified, and, by this our present charter, do confirm that grant and donation which umquhile Henry de Maule of Panmure made and granted to Alexander, son and heir of John of Strathachyn, and Christian, his daughter in free wedlock, of the lands of Carmyly, Drummadych, and Haewrangdrom, and half the lands of Achinlar, the mill and brew-house of Strathys, Caproshille, and Moncur, with their appurtenances. To be held by the said Alexander and Christian, and by their heirs, in fee and heirship in all their proper bounds and limits, together with all and sundry privileges, advantages, and easements, and just appanages whatever pertaining to said lands, mill and brew-house, or likely in any future time to pertain, as freely and fully, wholly and honourably, in all respects and throughout their whole extent, as the charter of the said Henry, at that time drawn up, rightly holds and bears; saving our service. We confirm also that sale which John of Glasleter made of one half of the lands of Awchinlar to the said Alexander of Strathachyn and of Carmyly: To be had and held by the said Alexander, his heirs and assignees, in fee and heirship, in all its proper limits and boundaries, together with all and sundry privileges, advantages, and easements, and just appanages whatever, belonging to the said lands and pasture lands with their appanages; or likely in any way in the future to pertain to him, as freely and fully, wholly and honourably, in all and every respect, as the charter of said John of Glasleter, at that time drawn out, justly bears and sets forth; saving our service. In witness whereof we have ordered the seal of our confirmation to be placed to the present charter: witnesses, the venerable fathers in Christ, William and John, our chancellor, bishops of St Andrews and Dunkeld; John, our eldest son of Carryk, seneschal of Scotland; Robert of Fyfe and Menteth, our beloved son; William of Douglas and of Mar, our cousin earl; James of Lindesay, our dearest nephew, and Robert Erskyn, our kinsman, knights. At Perth, 5th day of February, in the eleventh year of our reign" (Regist. de Panmure, vol. ii., pp. 179, 180).

During the reign of Robert III. (1390-1406), Alexander Strachan of Carmyllie received a royal charter of "ane annual out of the lands of Inglistoun, Brigtoun, and Kinnetlis" (Robertson's Index, 149, 40).

To Alexander Strachan, second of Carmyllie, was born a son, John, who, on the 17th June 1405, received the following royal charter, confirming to him a grant by William Maule of Panmure of the lands of Carmyllie and others:

"Robert, by the grace of God, King of Scots, to all honest men throughout his whole realm, clerks, and laity, greeting. *Know ye*, that we have approved, ratified, and, by this our present charter for ourselves and heirs, do for ever confirm to John of Strathachyn, son and heir of Alexander of Strathachyn, that gift and grant which umquhile William Maule of Panmure made and granted to the said John, of all and singly the lands of Carmyly, Drummadicht, Hachrangdrum, and Achlair, together with the pasture land and the white-hill mill and brewery, Strathys, Caproschill, and Moncur, with their appanages; which lands, mill, and brewery were the property of the said Alexander, and which the said Alexander, not constrained by force or fear, or beguiled into error, but out of his pure and spontaneous good will, resigned in whole and entirety into the hands of the said umquhile William, and invested him with right of stick and wood: To be had and held by the said John and his heirs in fee and heirship, in all these just bounds and limits, as fully and freely, wholly and honourably, thoroughly and without dispute in all and every respect, as the said Alexander freely held and possessed the said lands, mill, and brewery, with their appanages, before said resignation then made to the said William, save and except the usual service due to us and to our heirs for the said lands, mill, and brewery, with their appanages. In witness whereof we have ordered the seal of confirmation to be appended to this our present charter. Witnesses, the reverend father in Christ, Gilbert, bishop of Aberdeen, our chancellor; David Flemyng of Biggar, knight, our kinsman; John of Uchiltre; John of Crawfurd, our chaplain; and Angus de Camera, the chamberlain. At Linlithcu, 17th day of June 1405, and of our reign the 16th year" (Regist. de Panmure, vol. ii., pp. 185, 186).

On the 5th March 1500, David Strachan of Carmyllie endowed a chaplaincy at Carmyllie. In the charter of foundation he prohibited the monk from keeping a mistress, and provided that he should conduct a school for the education of the young. This charter was confirmed by James IV. in a royal charter, dated 20th January 1511 (Regist. de Panmure, vol. ii., pp. 263-267).

David Strachan of Carmyllie married Janet Drummond, by whom he became father of two sons, Alexander and James. On the 9th February 1508, a charter granted by David Strachan of Carmyllie to Alexander Strachan, his elder son, was, by Sir Thomas Maule of Panmure, confirmed in a charter, of which a translation follows:

"To all who shall see or hear this charter, Thomas Maule of Panmure, knight, lord superior of all and each the lands of Karmylie, greeting. Know ye that I have inspected and carefully examined, and fully understood, a certain charter of my beloved cousin, David Strathachyn of Karmyle, granted to Alexander Strathachyn, his son and heir-apparent, in regard to a perpetual grant and gift of all and sundry the lands of the demesne of Karmyle, with tenants, tenantries, and free services of tenants in the same, with pertinents, situated within the shire of Forfar and the barony of Panmure, sealed with the said David's seal, confirmed with red wax, a white impression hanging from the tail, free from erasures, cancellings, obliterations, mistakes, and, as it appears, unsuspected in any way, written on new parchment, and totally free from all error or ground of suspicion, as appears on the face of it, and to the following effect:

" 'To all who shall hear or see this charter, David Strathachyn of Karmyle, greeting. Know ye, that, moved with love of my son, I have given, granted, and, by this my present charter, do confirm, as well as by these presents, give, grant, and, by this my present charter, confirm to my very dear son and heir-apparent, Alexander Strathachyn, and to the male heirs who shall be lawfully begotten of his body; whom failing, to James Strathachyn, brother of the said Alexander, and his heirs-male whomsoever, the whole and entire lands of my demesne of Karmyle, with tenants and tenantries, and free services of tenants, together with the right of presentation and patronage of the chaplaincy of the chapel of the Blessed Virgin, situated within the said demesne, the same lying with their pertinents within the shire of Forfar and barony of Panmure: the said lands in my demesne of Karmyle, all and whole, to be had and held by the aforesaid Alexander, and his heirs-male who shall be lawfully begotten of his body; whom failing, by James Strathachyn, brother of the said Alexander, and his heirs-male whomsoever; from that noble man, Sir Thomas Maule of Panmure, knight, and his heirs, in blench fee and heirship for ever, according as they are thus defined: Beginning at the east from the western boundary of Kelly, and extending east as far as the eastern bank of the burn of Monquhir extends west; at the southern portion of the lands of Monquhir, as far as the boundaries extend; and from thence running north to the western angle of the Resyfald of Karmylie; and from thence extending as far as the ancient boundaries extend between the said lands of Karmyle and Glaster, to the western portion of the lands of Karmyle, called the Greystane; and from thence extending north to the layne between the Graystane and the Ridirfaldis, as far as the marks and bounds extend, touching the chapel on the west and south-west, and so up the burn towards the nave of the chapel; and thence north towards the northern part of the Ridirfaldis, and thence as far as the bounds and marks run in front of the highway; to the Red Fountain, and thence west, south-west, to the Moss of Dilto; and thence west to the boundary-stone between the lands of Panmure and Kirkbutho; and thence north to the south-western boundary of Tullo, and thence east as far as the green slaid extends on the north side of the Gallowhill, and so east to the south-western boundaries of the barony of Edwye, and thence east towards the south-western part of the lands of Beith; and thence south-west towards the south-western limits of the granges of Conan and Guthrie; and thence extending south-west as far as the boundaries extend between the lands of the barony of Kellie and the lands of Panmure, and up to the west bank of the burn of Monquhir aforesaid. Paying for the same yearly to the aforesaid noble gentleman, Sir Thomas Maule, one silver penny, current coin of the Scottish realm, as ground rent of said lands, by way of blench farm at the Feast of Pentecost, if such be demanded. Free holding, however, being reserved of all and sundry said lands, with their emoluments and gift of the chaplaincy of chapel aforesaid, to myself for the natural term of my life, and a reasonable third of the said lands being likewise reserved for Janet Drummond, my wife, and for any one else who may be my wife hereafter. In witness whereof my seal is appended to this my present charter at Dundee, 7th day of February 1508, in presence of these witnesses—Sir James Ochterlonie of yt. ilk, knight; James Wedderburn, burgess of Dundee; James Scrimgeour; Robert Sires, junior; Master Patrick Buttergask and Sir David Bell, notaries public; and several others.'

"Which charter of gift and concession, I confirm for ever. In witness whereof my seal of confirmation is appended to this my present charter, at the church of Moneykey, the 9th day of February, A.D. 1508, in presence of these witnesses foregoing—Alexander Strathachyn, brother-german of David Strathachyn of Karmyle; James Ochterlonie of Pitlewy; Sir John Mill, chaplain; Alexander Ramsay; John Fotheringam; John Affleck; William Allleck; Thomas Schankis; and Sir David Bell, notary public; with several others" (Regist. de Panmure, vol. ii., pp. 272-275).

Of the same date, Alexander Strachan, younger of Carmyllie, granted to Sir Thomas Maule of Panmure a bond of manrent of the following tenor:

"Be it kend till al men be ther presents, me Alex^{r.} Strauchan, son and ayr of David Stranchan of Carmylie, till be bund, oblist, and be the tenour of this present writt and the faith in my body, lellie and truellie binds and oblisses me and myne ayres till ane richt honourable man, Sir Thomas Maule of Panmure, knight, and his ayres, successouris and assignais; That forsamcikle as he has given to me confirmatioun vpoun my father's charter given to me of his lands of Carmylie, hereafter I become man and retainer, both in houshald and outwith houshald, till the said Sir Thomas, his heirs, successours, and assigneis; for eveir on my own expenses, when that he charges me to ryd or gang, and I sall take his afald and true pairt with my said maister in all his actions, causes, and quarrels monet, or to be monet be quhatsomevir person or persons in contrair to him; be firm and honest; and sall defend his person, heretages, lands, and gudes to all my gudelie power, but variance : and this my present bond of maurent and service in all points as is above written, I bind and obleis me and myne ayres and assignys, faithfully by the truth in my body, the haly Evangels touchit, lelely and truely till obsairve and keep and defend at all my gudelie power, to the said Sir Thomas, his ayres, successours, and assignays as said is, but (without) fraud, gyle, cavillation, or male (bad) engyne whatsomevir under the pain of the tinsall of my lands. In the witnes of the quhilk, becaus I have no seill proper of myne awin, I have procurit with instance the seill of ane honourable man, Hew Auchinleck of y^{t.} ilk, to be affixt to this my present bond of maurent, togedder with my subscription mannell, at Moneykey, the 9th day of Februar, the zeir of God on thowsand five hundert and aucht zeirs, befor thir witnesses—David Strauchin of Carmylie, my father; Alex^{r.} Strauchin; John Auchinleck; John Huntres; David Arbuthnot; and Sir David Bell, chaplain and notaires publict, with sundrie others. (Signed) ALEX^{n.} STRAUCHIN, *manu propria.*" (Regist. de Panmure, vol. ii., pp. 275, 276.)

The "Register of Panmure" contains the following lease, granted in 1524 by Robert Maule of Panmure to James Strachan, of part of the Eastertoun and mill of Guthrie:

"I, Robert Maule of Panmure, grantes me to have set to my luvit cusing, James Strathachin, and to his subtenentis, ane or many, all and haill the twelfe pairt of the landis of Estertoune of Guthre, and myln of the samyn, for all the termes of fyve yeiris, thair entres thairto beand at Whitsunday next; the said James or his subtenendis payand thairfore yeirlie in meil and custumes aucht and wonte, except xviij pultrie to be reservit to the said James. Subscrivet with my hand at Forfar, the 9 day of April and the yeir of God J^m V^c xxiiij yeiris" (Regist. de Panmure, vol. ii., p. 298).

By a royal letter, dated Falkland, 9th October 1540, Thomas Strachauchin, "son and heir of umquhile Alexander Strachauchin of Carmyle," received a gift of "the nonentres, males, fermes, etc., of all and sindry the landis of Carmyle, Skethin, Auchinlaw, and others lying in the barony of Panmure, within the sheriffdom of Forfar, which pertained to the said Alexander heritably, and were halden immediately of umquhile Thomas Mawle of Panmure, knight, excepting the said lands of Skethin, which were held immediately of Patrick Lord Gray, and which his father in like manner held of the said Thomas Mawle, all of which lands being now in the king's hands, by reason of non-entry, since the death of the said Sir Thomas Mawle" (Reg. Sec. Sig., vol. xiv., fol. 22; vol. xv., fol. 12*b*).

Thomas Strathauchin of Carmyllie is described as obtaining, on the the 12th December 1543, a decreet against "Thomas Strathauchin of Cairnton for non-entry duties out of the lands of Auchlare and Westerhills" (Regist. de Panmure. vol. ii., p. 308). On the 25th June 1557, a contract of marriage was executed between David Strachan, son of Thomas Strachan of Carmyllie, and Margaret, daughter of John Betoun of Auchinvoche, with consent of their fathers respectively (Reg. of Deeds, vol. i.). Isabella, eldest daughter of Thomas Strachan of Carmyllie, married John Thorntoun; their marriage-contract is dated at Newbotle, 23d July 1557, and among Thorntoun's curators are named "John Strathauchin of Claypottis" (Reg. Sec. Sig., vol. xxviii., fol. 83*b*). On the 3d December 1589, James Strathauchin of Carmyllie received from Patrick Maule of Panmure a precept of "clare constat," as heir of his great-grandfather's father, David Strathauchine of Carmyllie, in the lands of Skeichen in the barony of Panmure (Regist. de Panmure, vol. ii., p. 316).

In March 1593, a contract was entered into between Patrick Maule, younger of Panmure, Margaret Erskine, his spouse, and Elizabeth Maule, their daughter, on the one part, and James Strachan of Carmyllie on the other part, for the marriage of the said James and Elizabeth, in the prospect of which Patrick Maule engaged to infeft her in the lands of Skethin and others in liferent, and to provide a dowry of 4000 merks (Reg. of

Deeds, vol. lxxxi.). On the 29th July 1572, Patrick Strachan, brother to David Strachan of Carmyllie, obtained a respite for art and part of the slaughter of Alexander Gardin of Freak in September or October 1571 (Reg. Sec. Sig., vol. xi., fol. 116). Two other documents on the same subject are dated at Leith, 29th July 1572, and at St Andrews, 17th April 1574 (Reg. Sec. Sig., vol. xl., fol. 116*b*, and vol. xlii., fol. 79*b*). On the 4th June 1599, James Strachan of Carmyllie granted to Mr Gilbert Gardyne of Beth an obligation for 1600 merks, in complete payment of "tocher gude" with Isabel Strachan, sister of the said James, and now spouse to the said Mr Gilbert. One of the witnesses is Patrick Strachan, brother-german of the granter (Reg. of Deeds, vol. lxxv.). On the 11th February 1601, an obligation was granted by James Strachan of Carmyllie, as principal, and Alexander Strachan of Brigtoun and Gilbert Thornetoun, younger of that ilk, as cautioners, to pay to Isabel and Helen Strachan, daughters of the said James, 2000 merks each when they should be contracted in marriage after passing the age of fourteen, and providing that the said contracts should be approved by David Maxwell of Teling, Edward Rossy of that ilk, Alexander Strachan of Brigtoun, and Gilbert Strachan of Claypotts; and this in terms of the marriage-contract between the said James, their father, and Isabell Maxwell, his spouse, mother of the said Isabel and Helen, because they were without heirs-male of their bodies (Reg. of Deeds, vol. lxxvii.). In a contract, dated 25th April 1600, and witnessed by Patrick Strachan, brother of James Strachan of Carmyllie, the said James Strachan, as principal, and Alexander Strachan, younger of Brigtoun, and Gilbert Thornetoun of that ilk, cautioners, agree for 3000 merks to infeft Mr Robert Quhytlaw of Newgrange in the lands of Montquharie in the barony of Panmure (Reg. of Deeds, vol. lxxviii.).

On the 8th July 1609, the Privy Council acquitted several persons charged by James Strachan of Carmyllie and George Strachan of Skethin with having invaded the lands of the latter (Reg. Sec. Concilii, *Acta* 1609, fol. 703).

On the 11th July 1469, Robert Strachan and Alicia Browne, his wife, obtained from Sir Thomas Maule of Panmure a charter of the lands of Ballowsy (Balhousie) in the county of Forfar. Translated from the Latin, this charter is of the following import:

"Thomas Maule of Panmure, etc. Know ye, etc., that I have granted to Robert of Straythanchin and Alicia Broune, his wife, conjointly and individually, and to the survivor in conjoint fee, my whole lands of Ballowsy, in the barony of Panmure, which lands, with their appanages, belonged to the said Robert, and which the same Robert resigned into my hands: The said lands to be held by the said Robert and Alicia, his wife, or whosoever be the survivor, in conjoint fee, and by the heirs male and female, lawfully of them begotten, or who may be begotten; in default of whom, by the lawful and nearest heirs of said Robert whomsoever. The said Robert making thence annual return (and Alicia, his wife, or whosoever of them be survivor, and their heirs) of one pair of gloves at Ballowsy, at the Feast of Pentecost, as nominal blench farm, if such be required. In witness whereof my seal is appended to these presents, at the Monastery of Arbroath, the 11th July, A.D. 1469, in presence of these witnesses—the venerable Father Malcolm, by Divine grace abbot of said monastery; the most honourable and worthy Walter Stewart, lord of Lorne; the most honourable William de Achterlony of that ilk; and Sir John Guthrie, chaplain and notary public, with many others" (Regist. de Panmure, vol. ii., pp. 244, 245).

Robert Strachan of Balhousie is named in March 1509 as one of the bailies for infefting John Carnegie of Kinnaird and his wife in a portion of the lands of Coolistown, in the barony of Rescobie and county of Forfar (Fraser's Earls of Southesk, p. 23). A bond of manrent, dated at Panmure 12th January 1569, was granted by James and Robert Strachan of Balhousie to Thomas Maule of Panmure for a new infeftment to them in the lands of Balhousie (Regist. de Panmure, vol. ii., p. 314). On the 25th May 1602, John Strachan of Balwyssie (Balhousie) granted a bond of manrent to Patrick Maule of Panmure (Regist. de Panmure, vol. ii., p. 317). An instrument of resignation "ad remanentiam" of the lands of

Balhousie and others was granted by John Strachan of Balhousie in favour of Patrick Maule of Panmure, his superior (Regist. de Panmure, vol. ii., p. 318).

On the 28th May 1599, a contract was entered into between Robert Strachan of Balhoussie, with consent of Helen Carnegie, his spouse, on the one part, and Mr Andrew Drummond, minister at Panbride, on the other part, whereby for 2264 merks Robert Strachan disponed to Drummond "the shadow half" of Balhoussie, under reversion for the sum above named (Reg. of Deeds, vol. lxxii.). On the 31st May of the same year, Robert Strachan of Balhousie, with John Shepperd, his son-in-law, granted an obligation to Thomas Hunter, notary in Dundee, for 200 merks (Reg. of Deeds, vol. lxxv.). On the 26th January 1601, Andrew Fleschour, merchant-burgess of Dundee, granted an obligation to Robert Strachan of Balhousie, whereby, notwithstanding that "the said Robert had infeft the said Andrew in his lands of Balhousie irredeemably," yet the latter agreed to dispose of his rights to the lands, consenting to the sale of them by the said Robert to John Strachan of Claypotts (Reg. of Deeds, vol. lxxix.). On the 8th May 1601, a contract was subscribed at Dundee between John Strachan of Claypotts on the one part, and Robert Strachan of Balhousie, with consent of Helen Carnegie, his spouse, on the other part, for the sale by the latter to the former of the lands of Balhousie, under reversion for 2000 merks (Reg. of Deeds, vol. lxxxiii.).

In the Record of Gifts under the Privy Seal, is a precept dated 25th February 1511, for a remission to John Strachan "in the Claypottis," and five others, for the theft of seven horses and waggons from the lands of Kyncarins, over and nether, pertaining to the Chancellarie of Dunkeld, committed by them in company with Mr Gilbert Strachan, who asserted that the said Chancellarie belonged to him (Privy Seal Gifts, vol. iv.). Mr Gilbert Strachan was parson of Fettercairn. In the

Register of the Privy Seal is recorded a royal letter, dated at Edinburgh the 7th July 1527, granting to Master Gilbert Strachauchin, parsone of Fethircarne, prothonotar apostolic, etc., the gift of the ward, non entres, and releif of all landis and annuettis, etc., quhilkis pertenit to Charles Thornetoun of that ilk, etc., and als of the mariage of Archibald Thornetoun, etc. (Privy Seal Gifts, vol. v., fol. 70). Mr Gilbert Strachan is subsequently named as canon of Aberdeen (Privy Seal Gifts, vol. ix., fol. 47). He was succeeded as rector of Fettercairn and canon of Aberdeen by his nephew, Mr James Strachan or Strathauchin. This person, on the 4th April 1548, received a charter from Andrew Seytoun of Perbroith, of the shady half of the lands of Leuchland; which was confirmed under the Great Seal by Queen Mary, 9th April 1549 (Reg. Mag. Sig., lib. xxx. 422). On the 8th January 1558, Mr James Strathauchin, rector of Fettercairn, with consent of John, Archbishop of St Andrews, and the prior and convent thereof, granted a charter in favour of James Strathauchin, his nephew, and his heirs-male, etc., of the ecclesiastical lands of Chapeltoun, in the parish of Fettercairn, with a precept of sasine addressed to Patrick Strathauchin, his bailie. This charter was confirmed by James VI. in a royal charter, dated at St Andrews on the 6th August 1585 (Reg. Mag. Sig., xxxvi. 326). On the 14th August 1556, Thomas Maule of Panmure confirmed to Mr James Strachan, canon of Aberdeen, and his nephew, Gilbert Strachan, half the lands of Skryne (Reg. Mag. Sig., lib. xxxi. 330; Reg. Sec. Sig., vol. xxviii. 35*b*). Mr James Strachan, rector of Fettercairn, on the 6th August 1585, confirmed a charter of the lands of Chapelton, in the parish of Fettercairn, to James Strachan, his nephew on the brother's side, appointing Patrick Strachan as bailie to give sasine (Reg. Mag. Sig., lib. xxxvi. 326).

In the service of Thomas Maule as heir of his father, Robert Maule, in lands and mill of Cambystoun, dated 5th June 1560, expede at Forfar, the name of John Strathauchin of Claypotts occurs in the list of jury (Regist. de Panmure, vol. ii., pp. 309, 310). On the 7th and 18th September 1584, a marriage-contract was executed between Gilbert Strachan, younger of Claypotts, and Elizabeth, daughter of the late Alexander Maxwell of Tealing (Reg. of Deeds, vol. lxi.).

A branch of the family of Strachan settled at Musselburgh, near Edinburgh. Robert Strachan is, in 1645, styled "maltman in the Fisherraw and burgess of Musselburgh" (Reg. of Deeds, vol. 595, 8th February 1645). He had two sons, Robert and Archibald; and five daughters, Isabel, Janet, Elizabeth, Helen, and Margaret (Burgh Court Reg. of Musselburgh, May 1657). Robert Strachan, younger," indweller in Fisherraw," subscribed at Musselburgh, on the 30th December 1647, an obligation for 200 merks borrowed money (Reg. of Deeds, vol. 574). On the 20th July 1647, Robert Sandilands, merchant-burgess of Edinburgh, received, on behalf of "Major Archibald Strachan, sone lawful to Robert Strachan, burgess of Musselburgh," an obligation from David Christison for the loan of £1000 Scots. On the 24th November of the preceding year, Major Archibald Strachan received an obligation for 3000 merks from Robert Beattie, provost of Montrose, and his son, a burgess of Edinburgh (Reg. of Deeds, vol. 584).

Archibald Strachan was born at Musselburgh (Lamont's Diary, p. 27). In early life he abandoned himself to loose and profligate habits, but having amended his course of living, he joined the army of Cromwell at Preston (Baillie's Letters, iii. 112, 113). On the 29th May 1645, the English House of Commons ordered that Major Archibald Strachan "be forthwith sent for in safe custody" (Journals of House of Commons, iv. 156).

Archibald Strachane, "captain of the Parliament's army," as he is described, was on the 17th November 1643, present at the baptism of his nephew, Archibald, son of his sister, Isobel Strachan, by her husband, Thomas Smith, portioner of Inveresk (Baptismal Reg. of Inveresk). As an officer of the Scottish Parliament, he obtained distinction and inspired confidence. When the Marquis of Montrose landed in the north in 1650, Strachan, now lieutenant-colonel, and who had lately defeated General Middleton, was despatched with 300 cavalry to obstruct his progress, General David Leslie following with 4000 men (Malcolm Laing's History of Scotland, iii. 417). At Invercharran in Ross-shire, Montrose was surprised by Strachan on the 27th April 1650, and subjected to a total defeat. According to Sir James Balfour, Strachan was wounded in the engagement, but was able to pursue his routed antagonists for several miles. From the Scottish Parliament, on the 3d July 1650, he received a vote of thanks (Balfour's Annals, iv. 9, 10, 70). Till the death of Charles I., Strachan adhered to Cromwell. When Charles II., in June 1650, threw himself under the protection of the Scottish Parliament, Colonel Strachan keenly espoused the royal cause, and fought against the king's enemies. Commanding along with General Robert Montgomery 2000 cavalry and 500 foot, he defeated a party of Cromwell's troops at Musselburgh on the 31st July (Balfour's Annals, iv. 87). Before the close of the year, Colonel Strachan took command at Dumfries of the considerable army of the Remonstrants or Protesters, who objected to the young king on account of his not being a sound Covenanter. His withdrawal from the royal service was strongly resented; and at a meeting of the Estates on the 18th December, some members held that he should be denounced as a traitor. On Sunday the 12th January 1651, he was "excommunicated and delivered to the devil" in the church of Perth, by Mr Alexander Rollock; he was on the 20th March forfeited by Parliament, and his goods escheated to the king's use, by the following order:

"The King's Majestie and Parliament ordaines warrands and citations to be issued furth be the committee of billis for critting all and evrie on of the dettouris of Colonell Archibald Strauchane to compeir befoir the Parliament or Committee of Estaittis eftir the Parliament is rysin to heir and sie thame decernit to mak payment to the commissioneris of the thesaurie for his Majesties use of sic soumes of money as they ar auchtand to the said Colonell Strauchane. And the Estaittis of Parliament declairis that the discharges to be granted to the saidis debtouris be the commissioneris of the thesaurie, of the saidis soumes shalbe valeid and sufficient discharges to warrand the saids debtouris at the hands of the said Colonel Strauchane, and all others having interesse. In respect it is notourlie knowin to the Estaittis that the said Coll. Strauchane is gone in to the publick enemy of this kingdome " (Acta Parl. Scot., vol. vi., p. 586).

According to Sir James Balfour (Annals), Colonel Strachan was forfeited for "betraying the country to sectaries." This charge, which implied that he had re-attached himself to Cromwell, was without foundation. He remained true to the Presbyterians, and when Cromwell offered him the command of all his forces in Scotland, he declined the offer. Possessed of deep religious fervour, the sentence of excommunication pronounced against him at Perth deeply moved him, and shortened his life (Wodrow's Analecta, ii. 86). He was addicted to melancholy, on account of his early errors (Baillie's Letters).

In the Burgh Court Book of Musselburgh, under date 7th May 1655, is the following entry: "Isobel Strachane, with consent of Thomas Smyth, portioner of Inveresk, her spouse, Janet, Bessie, Helene, and Margaret Strachanes, all lawful sisters, and appeirand executrices to umq^{le} Colonell Archibald Strachane, in favour of Robert Strachane, baillie, their brother, of all that they could claim of goods, money, etc., in terms of the testament of the said umq^{le} Colonell Archibald Strachane."

Isobel Strachan, eldest sister of Colonel Archibald Strachan, was first wife of Thomas Smith, portioner of Inveresk, to whom she bore thirteen children (Baptismal Reg. of Inveresk). Another of the sisters married Mr Thomas Warner, minister of Balmaclellan, who was deprived in 1662 by the government of Charles II. (Fasti Eccl. Scot., vol. i., 695).

On the 3d February 1653, William Strachan, described as "indweller in Fisherrow, burgess of Musselburgh, granted an obligation to Bailie John Henderson for 110 merks Scots of borrowed money, Robert Strachan, sumtyme baillie of Mussellbrught," being cautioner (Reg. of Deeds, vol. 611).

Alexander Strathachin de Balmaddie was member of an inquest, which assembled at Dundee on the 16th May 1508, for serving John Carnegie of Kinnaird heir to his father in the lands of Kinnaird and Little Carcary (Fraser's Earls of Southesk, p. 524). Of an inquest held at Dundee on the 7th November 1513 for serving Robert Carnegie of Kinnaird heir to John Carnegie his father, in the lands of Kinnaird, James Strathachin of Balmaddie was one of the members (Fraser's Earls of Southesk, p. 24).

A branch of the House of Strachan possessed the lands of Kinnetles in the county of Forfar. Alexander Strathachin de Kynnetles is named on an inquest, which, on the 28th April 1483, served Walter Rothven heir of his mother, Euphame Stewart, in the half lands of Lunan (Fraser's Earls of Southesk, p. 522).

In the retour of the service of Alexander Lyndsay, as heir to his father, Richard Lyndsay of the Smithy, of the lordship of Brechin, dated 29th April 1514, Alexander Strathachin de Brigtoune, in the parish of Kinnetles, is named as one of the inquest.

On the 6th February 1516, Alexander Strachan, as nephew and heir of Alexander Strachan, received a precept for a charter of the barony of Brigton and Kynnettles (Reg. Sec. Sig., vol. iii., fol. 53). He is mentioned as member of inquest in the service, 13th April 1532, of William Tyre, as heir to his grandfather, Walter Tyre, in half the lands of Lunan (Fraser's Earls of Southesk, p. 528). At Dundee, on the 12th April 1597, Thomas Strachan, brother-german to Alexander Strachan of Brigton, granted a bond for £100 to William Newton, burgess of Dundee (Reg. of Deeds, vol. lxxii.). On the 29th December 1561, a charter was granted to Alexander Strachan, nephew and heir-apparent of Alexander Strachan of Brigton of Kynnetles, upon the resignation of the latter, reserving his liferent (Reg. Sec. Sig., vol. xxx., fol. 76). On the 17th January 1574-5, Alexander Strachan, described as above, and Elizabeth Arbuthnot, his spouse, received a precept for a charter of the lands of Inglistoun of Kynnettles, on resignation of the said Alexander Strachan, junior (Reg. Sec. Sig., vol. xxxii., fol. 129). On the 4th December 1600, Alexander Strachan, younger of Brigtoun, and Gilbert Thorntone, apparent of that ilk, granted a discharge of a bond of 500 merks (Reg. of Deeds, vol. lxxxiv.). On the 29th November 1610, an Act was passed for apprehending him for a debt of 3000 merks (Acts of Secret Council, vol. 1610-12, fol. 33).

Alexander Strachan, younger of Brigtoun of Kinnetles, died in November 1613. From the Commissariat Register we obtain the following abstract of his testament-dative and inventory:

"The *Testament-dative* & *Inventarie* of the guidis and geir of umquhill Alexander Strachanchin, fear of Brigtoun, within the parochin of Kynnetillis and shirefdome of Forfar, the tyme of his deceis, quha deceissit in the moneth of November 1613 yeiris, ffaythfullie maid and gevin up be Elizabeth Ochterlony, his relict spons, in name of Robert and Patrick Strachanchinis, their lauchfull bairnes and executoures-datives, decernit to him be decreit of the commisar of St Andrews, the xx day of Januar 1614.

" In the first, twa old hors price x lib.,   .   . Summa, xx lib.
" Item, twa ky ; price of the pece, xij lib.,   .   ,,   xxiiij lib.
" ,,   ten auld scheip; price of the pece, xs.,   .   ,,   xx ,,
" ,,   in vtincillis and domicillis, estimat to   .   .   xx merkis

Summa of the Inventarie,   lxxix lib. vis. viijd.

" Na debtes awand to the deid nor be him.
" —Quota, xxvs. viijd.—To be devydit in twa partis ; ilk partis xxv lib. xvs. ijd.
" The present inventarie aboue-written, Together with the executoures thairin constitut, is confirmat vpoun the xvj day of August 1614 : the said Elizabeth Ochtiriony maid

fayth, etc. And Mr Daniel Lindesay, minister of Kynnettillis, is becum cautioun, &c." (Com. Reg. of St Andrews, vol. v.).

About the year 1343, Donald Strathechin and Annabell, his wife, received from David II. a charter of the lands of Kingstour, Landleyis, and Godefraystoune, in the county of Forfar, resigned into the king's hands at Barbrothe by Andrew Burr; and on 16th April 1343, the lands of Cardenbarclay, and annual furth of the miln of Panmure, county of Forfar; also the barony of Monycabbock, Tullimaddin, and Craig, in the county of Aberdeen (Robertson's Index, p. 48, No. 34). Donald Strachan and his wife Annabell had an only daughter, Christian, who married Sir Malcolm Fleming of Biggar, ancestor of the noble House of Wigton (Playfair's Baronetage).

According to Playfair, Donald Strachan was elder son of Sir James Strachan and Agneta de Thornton; he inherited the lands of Thornton, in which he was succeeded by his younger brother John, who was knighted by Robert II. His successor in the lands of Thornton was Alexander Strachan, who, if we accept the authority of Playfair, was his son or nephew (Playfair's Baronetage, vol. iii., p. 167). Alexander Strachan of Thornton is named as witness to a charter of the lands of Torwood in 1414. As "Alexander de Strathachin domino de Ladynkirk," he is mentioned as witness in a notarial instrument, on the 9th July 1434, relative to the bishop of Brechin's right to a portion of the Moss of Monrenmont, called Wellflat. To a charter by John Clerkson to Walter de Carnegy of a portion of the lands of Little Carkary, dated 8th January 1438, is attached the seal of "Alexander de Strathechyn, lord of Thornton," in substitution for the granter's, who had no seal. As witnesses are named Alexander de Strathechyn and James de Strathechyn (Fraser's Earls of Southesk, p. 514).

Alexander Strachan of Thornton married Margaret, daughter of John

Hay of Tillibothy and Enzie, by whom he had a son who bore the same Christian name. Alexander Strachan, the younger, succeeded to the patrimonial estate: he married Margaret, daughter of —— Rose of Kilravock, and had a son, John, his successor (Playfair's Baronetage).

John Strachan or Strathachin of Thornton was witness to a charter granted by James IV., on the 5th February 1473, to George Strathachin of Lesmorchie; in the year following he obtained a charter of the lands of Thornton, and the lands of Wismanstoun, Myrtoun, and Pitgervy. On the 5th March 1487, he executed an entail of his estate on his sons and heirs-male, whom failing, on his own nearest heirs-male whatsoever, bearing the name and arms of Strachan (Playfair's Baronetage). According to the Macfarlane MSS. (Advocates Library), he married Margaret, daughter of —— Straiton of Lauriston, an old family in Kincardineshire, by whom he had two sons. Probably Margaret Straiton was his first wife; for it would appear that the wife of John Strachan of Thornton in 1503 was Janet Ross, to whom is reserved in that year (Playfair) "a reasonable third part" of the lands of Thornton. He had five sons—David, his successor; John, who married Margaret, daughter of Sir William Durham of Grange; William, who founded the family of Strachan of Monboddo, in the parish of Fordoun, Kincardineshire; Andrew and George.

David Strathachin or Strachan of Thornton was Receiver-General for the Thanage of Kincardine from 1480 to 1482 (Exchequer Rolls). He was Justice-Clerk, that is, clerk of the Justiciary Court, from 1492 to 1497. He is thus referred to in the Treasurer's Accounts, p. 80: "Item the xxii° Novembris to Ormond to passe in the Northland to proclaime the Ayris (Justice Airs), iij[lb.] Item to Dave Strachawchin, Justis Clerk, to passe to resave the dittay thare, iiij[lb.]" On the 6th January 1500, he received confirmation of two charters of the lands of Thornton;

also the lands of Polgarvy, Muirtoun, Wisemanstoun, and two parks at Kincardine (Reg. Sec. Sig., vol. ii., fol. 136). He married Margaret Hay, daughter of William, fifth Earl of Errol. On the 4th December 1512, he and his wife received a royal charter of the lands of Brigtoun, in the barony of Thornton (Privy Seal Register, vol. iv., fol. 207). On the 2d June 1517, he mortified four merks of annual rent in augmentation of the chaplaincy founded by him in the parish church of Aberluthnot, or Marykirk, in honour of the Virgin (Privy Seal Register, vol. v., fol. 110). In an instrument by William, Bishop of Aberdeen, dated 10th December 1517, and annexing the hospital and church of Aberluthnot to the University of Aberdeen, he is styled "David Strathauchin filio et apparente herede domini de Thornetoune" (Records of King's College).

Having no children of his own, David Strachan made, in 1521, a formal resignation of his estate in favour of his nephew Alexander, elder son of his younger brother John, reserving his own liferent, that of his wife and of his brother John, and of his wife Margaret Durham (Playfair's Baronetage). John Strachan, younger son of John Strachan and Margaret Durham, obtained the lands of Duliewardis, in which he was succeeded by a son John, and a grandson John. The last married Elizabeth Lechtown (Reg. Mag. Sig., lib. xxxix. 87, 17th July 1593).

Alexander Strachan of Thornton, who succeeded his uncle David, occupies a somewhat prominent position in reference to an event of no ordinary interest. He was one of Queen Mary's "justiciars," appointed to make trial of George, Earl of Rothes, on the charge of being privy to the murder of Cardinal Beaton, in which were concerned his son, Norman Leslie, and John Leslie, his brother. The appointment of Alexander Strachan as a "justiciary," and his procedure in that office, are thus set forth in the Fourth Report of the Historical Commissioners.

Among the documents preserved in the charter room of the Countess of Rothes, at Leslie House, Fifeshire, the commissioners found a commission by Queen Mary, proceeding upon the narrative that

"Her Majesty's cousin, George, Earl of Rothes, Lord Leslie, had been delated several times, as well before his going to Hungary as since his return, to her Majesty's dearest cousin and tutor, James, Earl of Arran, Lord Hamilton, protector and governor of the kingdom, and to the lords of the Privy Council, by the bad reports of his enemies, that the Earl was under suspicion of the cruel and treasonable murder of David, Cardinal Archbishop of St Andrews, chancellor of the kingdom, and for taking and retaining, contrary to her Majesty's authority, of the castle of St Andrews, where the son and heir-apparent of her dearest cousin and tutor then was. And therefore her Majesty's said tutor and governor thought it expedient that the said Earl should be put to the knowledge of an assize for these things: Wherefore her Majesty made, constituted, and ordained Mr Alexander Strachanchin of Thornton, David Murray of Balvaird, knight, and another, or any one of them, jointly or severally, her Majesty's justiciars in that part, to call and accuse by indictment the said George, Earl of Rothes, for being art and part of the foresaid treasonable murder, and taking and detaining of the said castle of St Andrews, where the son and heir of her Majesty's said tutor was for the time."

The commission is dated at Peebles the 12th of July 1547, the principal being signed by the Lord Governor. Upon the back it bears that

"At the Water of Yarrow, on the 15th of July 1547, in presence of the said governor and George, Earl of Huntly, Lord Gordon and Badenoch, lord chancellor of Scotland, compeared personally the said Mr Alexander Strachanchin, and accepted the foresaid office of justiciar in that part anent the execution of the foresaid commission, having sworn upon the holy Evangells faithfully to administer justice in the above matter: Whereupon the said George, Earl of Rothes, asked and took instruments: Under the hand of John Wallace, notary public."

Also preserved in Leslie House is a

"*Testimonial* made out by way of instrument by Mr Alexander Strachanchan, bearing that the Earl of Rothes had compeared in judgment before him in a court of justiciary, held by him, in the fields near the Water of Yarrow, in the presence of the Lord Governor and Lord Chancellor, which Earl of Rothes stood indicted, and by the Queen's Rolls, was accused of being art and part of the treasonable murder of the most reverend David, Cardinal Archbishop of St Andrews, he, being then Chancellor of the kingdom, in the month of May

1546, giving his counsel and advice to Normond Leslie, Master of Rothes, his son, John Leslie, his brother, and to other persons who had committed the said treasonable homicide, with their own hands, by the command and assistance of the said Earl, and of the said treasonable assistance, favour, help of the said persons in the treasonable taking of the Castle of St Andrews at the same time; and keeping the said castle ever since, supplying them with victuals, munitions, and other necessaries; and in the treasonable assistance, favour, counsel, and help, given to the said persons at the time foresaid, in taking the said castle, where the said Lord Governor's eldest son and heir-apparent then was, and who was the third person of the kingdom, and detaining him in captivity ever since; as also for his treasonable correspondence with them and their accomplices, rebels to the Queen, for the said treasonable murder, and being at the house; and so being partaking with them in their treasonable deeds. Which deeds, calumnies, and crimes, the said George, Earl of Rothes, altogether denied in face of court, and by a condign assize was acquitted, and altogether freed of the said crimes. In Testimony Whereof the said justiciar subscribed and affixed his seal to the foresaid certificate, as did likewise Robert Carnegie of Kinnaird, and John Wallace, notary public, clerks to the said justiciary court at the fields near the Water of Yarrow, the said 15th of July 1547." (Report of Historical Commissioners, part iv., p. 504).

Alexander Strachan married, first, Margaret Hay of Dalgety, and secondly, Isabel Falconer of Halkerton (Macfarlane's MSS.). He left an only son, John, his successor, and four daughters. The eldest daughter espoused Wood of Balbegno; Margaret married, first, William Ramsay of Balmain, and secondly, Ogston of Ogston; Jean married Henry Graham of Morphie (Macfarlane's MSS.). Elizabeth married Andrew Arbuthnot of Pitcarles, fourth son of Robert Arbuthnot of that ilk. Alexander Arbuthnot, her second son, born in 1538, was the first Principal of King's College, Aberdeen, after the Reformation; he died in 1583 (Innes's Sketches of Early Scotch History, p. 283). On the 1st June 1548, William Ramsay of Balmain was confirmed in the Mains of Balmain, Ramsay Strath, and Mill of Fettercairn, in the barony of Balmain, for which he had received a charter from the late Alexander Strachan of Thornton (Reg. Sec. Sig., vol. xxii., fol. 4).

In the Records of the Privy Seal (vol. xvii., fol. 79; Reg. Mag. Sig., lib. xxix. 61) is contained a precept for confirmation of a charter by Alexander Strachan of Thornton to John Strachan, his son and apparent heir, and Margaret Livingstoun,[1] his spouse, of the lands of Newbigging, Huntersett, Boghall, and others, dated 12th April 1543. In the same Records (vol. xviii., fol. 97) is a precept for remission to Alexander Strachan of Thornton and twenty-one others for treasonably assisting Archibald, Earl of Angus, Matthew, Earl of Lennox, and William, Earl of Glencairn, and their accomplices, in their insurrection against the Lord Regent at Leith, dated at Edinburgh 8th November 1544.

In the beginning of the sixteenth century, Thomas Strachan owned the castle and lands of Lenturk, in the parish of Leochel, Aberdeenshire. The castle of Lenturk is described by Monipennie in 1612 (Brief Description of Scotland), as one of the strongholds of Mar. In 1792 it appeared as an extensive ruin, surrounded by a deep hard fosse (Sinclair's Stat. Acct.). "John Strachan, younger of Lethinturk," with several others received, on the 26th April 1536, a royal pardon for the slaughter of Alexander Seton of Meldrum. On the 20th July 1537, he obtained from James V., a conditional remission of his having participated in the Master of Forbes's treason in attempting the king's life [2] (Pitcairn's Criminal Trials, vol. i., pp. 175-200). On the 4th December, 1549 he received "a respite" for "treasonably remaining from the army at Pinkie Cleuch, in September 1547, to last for nineteen years." In this instrument he is described as "John Strachan, son and heir of the late Thomas Strachan of Lenturkis" (Reg. Sec. Sig., vol. xxvi., fol. 30). On the 13th April 1546, he was confirmed in the lands of Lenturk, which were constituted into a free barony (Privy Seal Records, vol. xx., fol 9). Of these lands and the barony he made a disposition in favour of John Strachan of Thornton, who, on the 24th July 1548, received confirmation of his charter, reserv-

---

[1] A daughter of Livingston of Dunipace (Pedigree by John Withie, Harleian MSS., 1423).
[2] The Master of Forbes was beheaded on the 14th June of the same year.

ing the granter's free life interest (Reg. Sec. Sig., vol. xxii., fol. 4). On the 27th May 1552, John Strachan of Thornton received gifts of the escheat of John Strachan of Lenturk, and Sir John Cristeson, notary, both at the horn (Reg. Sec. Sig., vol. xxv., fol. 2b). On the 22d March 1553, he with some others received a remission for being absent from the battle of Pinkie Cleuch (Reg. Sec. Sig., vol. xxvi., fol. 81b).

On the 29th June 1553, John Strachan and Margaret Livingston, spouses, received precept for a charter of the lands of Brigtoun, in the barony of Thornton, on the resignation of the former. In 1560 John Strachan received the lands of Haddow in the parish of Conveth (Laurencekirk), Kincardineshire, which had belonged to the Priory of St Andrews, and were confirmed to him under the Great Seal, 23d November 1570 (Privy Seal Register, vol. xxxix., fol. 51; Reg. Mag. Sig., lib. xxxii. 66). On the 20th December 1567, John Strachan of Thornton and Margaret Livingston, his spouse, received, from William, Bishop of Aberdeen, confirmation of a charter of the lands of Innoquhuly, which belonged to the late Alexander Strachan of Thornton, father of the said John; Andrew Strachan, brother-german of the said John is a witness (Reg. Mag. Sig., lib. xxxvii. 393). John Strachan sat in Parliament in the year 1560, when the Reformed doctrines were publicly ratified. On the 31st October 1570, he became surety for David Strathauchin at the Mylne of Thornetoune, and others charged with the slaughter of Peter Rait (Pitcairn's Criminal Trials, vol. i., p. 17). On the 23d November 1570, he received a precept for confirmation of a charter, from James, Commendator of the Priory and Monastery of St Andrews, of the lands of Haddow and Lawsched in the parish of Conveth and shire of Kincardine (Reg. Sec. Sig., vol. xxxix., fol. 51). He obtained on the 8th March 1573-4, a gift of the non-entry of the lands of Culquhorsy, Kirktoun of Echt, etc., in the barony of Cluny and shire of Aberdeen, in the king's hands since the death of George, Earl of Huntly (Reg. Sec. Sig., vol. xlii., fol. 20). On the 30th June 1577, he had a gift of the ward and non-entry of the lands of Knockquharne and others in the shire of Aberdeen (Reg. Sec. Sig., vol. xliii., fol. 110).

When the Duke of Chatelherault, better known as the Regent Arran, claimed the regency as by right of blood, after the battle of Langside, he held a pretended parliament within the Tolbooth of Edinburgh, on the 29th August 1571, at which he forfeited those opposed to his pretensions. Among those enumerated are —— Straquhane of Thorneton, and —— Straquhane, his sone and appeirand air (Diurnal of Occurrents, p. 243).

John Strachan of Thornton was present in the Parliament held at Edinburgh, 24th November 1572, when the Earl of Morton was elected Regent (Acta Parl. Scot., iii. 77); two years afterwards he was appointed commissioner for Kincardineshire to superintend the making of "wappingshawingis," then ordered to be held twice a year throughout the kingdom (Acta Parl. Scot., iii. 91). He died at Aberdeen, 20th August 1587 ("Chronicle of Aberdeen," Miscellany of Spalding Club, ii. 59), leaving one son, Alexander, and three daughters, Elizabeth, Helen, and Jean.

John Strauchauchin "in Kincragy," barony of O'Neill, Aberdeenshire, was, on the 18th July 1548, declared "to be escheated for his remaining at hame, and being absent fra the first sege of Sanctandrois" (St Andrews) (Reg. Sec. Sig., vol. xxii., fol. 20). On the 11th August 1546, he received "the gift of his own escheat, for remaining at home from the last raid of Haddington" (Reg. Sec. Sig., vol. xxii., fol. 25b).

On the 6th November 1562, Patrick Forbes of Corse obtained confirmation of a charter, by which he granted the lands of Kyneragy in liferent to Elizabeth, daughter of John Strachan of Thornton (Privy Seal Register, vol. xxxi., fol. 112); and on the 30th December 1569, confirmation was granted to a charter by John Forbes, lord of the fee of the lordship of Aicht (Echt), with consent of Robert Forbes, his grandfather, and others, his curators, in favour of Helen, daughter of John Strachan of Thornton, in liferent, of the lands of Cowlie in the barony of Aicht (Privy Seal Register, vol. xxxviii., fol. 112).

John Strachan of Thornton left no will. In his testament-dative and inventory, recorded in the Commissariat Register of Edinburgh (vol. xix., 21st May 1588), he is described as "a rycht honorabill man, Johne Strauchanchin, laird of Thornetoun, in the Mernis," and his only executor is his son and heir, "the rycht honorabill Alexander Strauchanchin, laird of Thornton." The amount of his inventory is £4339, 1s. 8d., with debts due to him amounting to £860, 16s. 8d.

On the 20th November 1553, Alexander Strachan of Brigtoun (younger of Thornton) obtained licence "to remove and byde at hame fra . . . oitis (jousts), armys, raids, gadderings, and wappinshawingis," etc., for his lifetime, and to be free from all appearance before judges, spiritual and temporal, sitting on inquests (Privy Seal Register, vol. xxvi., fol. 25).

On the 15th December 1586, a charter was confirmed by Alexander Strachan, "fear of Thornetoun," with consent of John Strachan, freeholder thereof, to Robert Strachan, eldest son and apparent heir of the said Alexander and Sara Dowglas, his spouse, of the lands of Caldame, Mid-Mains of Thornetoun, etc., and to the said Sara in liferent of the lands of Hauchhead and Braidisleis (Privy Seal Register, vol. liv., fol. 153).

Alexander Strachan of Thornton received on the 30th August 1588 a charter of *nocodamus* of the lands and barony thereof (Privy Seal Register, vol. lviii., fol. 16). On the 29th October 1590, he obtained confirmation of charters of the lands of Innoqulne and others in the county of Aberdeen, which belonged to "the late John Strachan of

Thornetoun and Margaret Levingston, his spouse" (Privy Seal Register, vol. lxi., fol. 64). A precept for a charter was, on the 19th December 1590, granted to Alexander Strachan of Thornton, of the lands of Scheilling of Auchanbrak, etc., which belonged "to the late Mr Alexander Strachan of Thornetoun, grandfather of the granter" (Privy Seal Register, vol. iv., fol. 126). On the 18th August 1592, he received a gift of the castle of Kincardine (Privy Seal Register, vol. lxiv.). On the 12th February 1601, he obtained a second charter of *novodamus* of the barony of Thornton (Privy Seal Register, vol. lxxi., fol. 371).

Alexander Strachan married, first, Isabel, daughter of William, fourth Earl Marischal, who died in August 1595; secondly, Anna, daughter of Laurence Mercer of Meikleour, relict of James Learmonth of Balcomie, who after his decease married as her third husband ~~Alexander Gowan of Lismore~~ (Withie's Pedigrees, Harleian MSS., 1423).

On the 9th January 1600, Anna Mercer, second wife of Alexander Strachan, obtained sasine of the lands of Newbigging and others in the parish of Fettercairn in liferent (Register of Sasines, vol. i., fol. 4). In April and May 1601, she received sasine for her liferent interest of other lands belonging to the Thornton estates.

Alexander Strachan of Thornton was predeceased by Robert, his eldest son, who died sometime prior to 1596. Alexander Strachan died in May 1601. His testament and inventory were "given up by Anna Mercer, his relict spous, and John Strathauchin, his sone," executors "appointed by the defunct" (Edinburgh Commissariat Register, vol. xxxvii., 5th August 1602). The amount of his inventory was £3517, 6s. 8d., with debts due to him amounting to £1088, 16s. 8d. Among the debts due by him were £9, 13s. 4d. to "James Strauchin of Monboddo, for the fens of Fettercairn and Fordoun for 1601; and to William Strauchan of Tulliefroskie, for half ane year's annual rent furth of the defunctis lands of Kincardine, resten in anno 1601, ten bollis, feir price of the boll V lib—L lb." By his will he gave his body to be buried "in my ile in Mariekirk, in the card fra quhence it came." He bequeathed 200 merks "to be wairit upon land" for the support of the "waik and pure and bedrells of the parochyne of Abirlichmat" (Marykirk). He ordained Anna Mercer, his spouse, and "John Strauchan," his son, to "enterteyn and gif household to David Trumbill, George Nydrie, Johne Gordoun, elder, Johne and Johne Adames, John Gaw, elder, and Christian Irving, sa lang as the said Anna and Johne remaynes in household togidder, and fra they dissolve cumpany to gif everie ane of thame ane peck of meill ouklie (weekly) quhill Alexander Strauchane, my oy and air, be evadit twenty-ane yeiris, at quhilk tyme he sal be astrictit to gif thame and ilk ane of thame ane peck victuall during thair liftimes." He further provided that his wife was to reside at Thornton along with his son John, and that his three unmarried daughters, Magdalen, Katherine, and Elizabeth, were to remain with his wife until their respective marriages. His will is dated 14th May 1601, and the witnesses are Robert Mercer in Craiggis, George Strauchan, the testator's "sone," Alexander Strachauman in Arnebarrow, and Robert Mylne, notary.

Alexander Strachan of Thornton was father of three sons, Robert, John, and George, and four daughters, Jean, Magdalen, Katherine, and Elizabeth.[1] On the 6th February 1593, Alexander Strachan of Thornton and Jean his daughter on the one part, and Alexander Tulloch of Craignestoun and David Tulloch, eldest son of the late Andrew Tulloch in Odmainstoun, and apparent heir of the said Alexander Tulloch, on

---

[1] According to Withie (Harleian MSS., 1423), the sons of Alexander Strachan—Robert, John, and George—were born of his first marriage, and his daughters of his second marriage. Jean was certainly of the first marriage.

the other part, entered into a contract for the marriage of the said David and Jean. Alexander Strachan bound himself to pay to his daughter 3500 merks of tocher (Reg. of Deeds, vol. xciii.). Of the younger daughters, Magdalen married William Rait of Halgreen; Katherine married John Middleton of Killhill, Kincardineshire; and Elizabeth married William Forbes of Corse, Aberdeenshire.

Robert Strachan, eldest son of Alexander Strachan of Thornton, predeceased his father. He married, on the 4th April 1586, Sara, daughter of Sir William Douglas of Glenbervie, afterwards ninth Earl of Angus, who after his death espoused as her second husband Sir George Auchinleck of Balmanno (Withie's Pedigrees, Harleian MSS., 1423). On the 1st March 1597, a contract respecting the exchange of certain lands was entered into between Alexander Strachan of Thornton on the one part, and Sara Douglas, relict of Robert Strachan, son and heir-apparent of the said Alexander Strachan, with consent of George Auchinleck of Balmanno, now her spouse, on the other part (General Register of Deeds, vol. lv.).

Alexander Strachan, only child of Robert Strachan and his wife Sara Douglas, and described in the will of Alexander Strachan of Thornton as his "oy (grandson) and air," became of age in 1606. On the 30th September of that year, he is retoured heir-male to Alexander Strathauchan of Thornton, his paternal grandfather, in the lands and barony of Thornton and other lands (Inquisit. Special., Kincardine, 18). On the 7th April 1613, he had a charter of the lands of Newbigging, and the patronage of the church of Fetteresso (Privy Seal Register, vol. lxxxi., fol. 190). In September of the same year, he and John and George Strachan, his uncles, Dr Robert Strachan, physician in Montrose, and others, were charged before the Privy Council, at the instance of the King's Advocate, for assailing Captain Alexander Wishart of Phesdo, and forcibly depriving him of a legal instrument. The proceedings, as detailed in the Privy Council Register, are subjoined :—

"*Apud Edinburgh xv. die mensis Septembris* 1613.

"Anent oure soueraine lordis lettres reasit at the instance of Sir William Oliphant of Newtoun knycht his maiesteis aduocat for his heynes interesse and Capitane Alexander Wischart of Faisdo makand mention That quhairvpoun the sevintene day of August instant the said Captain Alexander being with Alexander Strauchane of Thornetonn in his awne place of Thornetoun and in tyme of denner being in conference with him anent the tak of the teyndis of the landis of Pittarrow and some vtheris landis perteining to the said Capitane Alexander that mater at the desyre of the said Laird of Thornetoun wes continewit to the nynetene day of August instant and he earnestlie intreatit the said Capitane to come bak to his house that day and he sould haif the tak dewlie formitt and deliuerit to him vpoun suche reasonnable conditionis as sould content him And the said Capitane Alexander lippyning to his promeis and looking for nothing les than ony violence or iniurie to haue bene attemptit aganis him be the said Laird of Thornetoun with whom so laitlie afoir he pairtit in so freindlie termes of love and freindschip The said Capitane Alexander addressit him selff in peciable and quiet maner accompanyed onlie with his thrie domesticq servandis towardis the said Alexanderis house and approcheing neir the same being alwyse vpoun his awne ground and heritage the said Capitane Alexander persauit him selff inuironed about on all sydis be a nomber of men convocat and assemblit togidder be the said Alexander Strauchane being in nomber auchtene personis and airmed with hagbutis and pistolletis prohibite to be worne be the Lawis of this realme, of the quhilk nomber the personis vndirwrittin wer chief and principall Thay ar to say the said Alexander Strauchane Johnne and George Straquhanis his vnclis Mr Robert alis doctor Straquhan Adam Straquhan sone to vmquhill [*blank*] Straquhan of Glenkindi Gilbert Conch at the mylne of Boguidoloche Alexander Straquhan thair Walter Pikisman seruitour to the said Laird of Thornetoun Robert Irving in Quitstane Robert Straquhan sone to William Straquhan sumtyme in Muirailhous and Alexander Straquhan at the mylne of Glendi, who haueing twapet about the said Capitane Alexander maid him to licht frome his horse seaueing as appeirit to . . . . purpois foirsaid anent the tak of the teyndis and the rest of Thornetonne: company haueing sinderit the said Capitanis servandis frome him the said Laird of Thornetoun him selff accompanyed with the saidis Johnne and Robert Straqnhanis his vnclis and Mr Robert Straquhan quha is callit Doctor Straquhan attending the said Capitane Alexander and forgetting the formair purpois and conference anent the teyndis the said Laird of Thornetoun in a verie presumptuous and boisting maner cravit frome the said Capitane Alexander ane lettre of dischairge and renunciatioun past of ony tyme before betuix the said Capitane Alexander and Margaret Straquhan sister to the said Laird of Thornetoun, and the said Capitane Alexander at the first refnising to mak deliuerie thairof the said Laird and his complicis foirsaidis all in a voce with mony horrible aithis to haue his lyif gif he maid nat present deliuerie of the said renunciatioun quhilk forme of behauour being verie vneouth and strange vnto the said Capitane Alexander and being closit about with a nomber of airmed men and sinderit frome his awne company The said Capitane Alexander tauld thame as the treuth wes that he could not mak present deliuerie of the said lettre althocht thay sould tak his lyff becaus it wes in his chairtour kist in his house of Balfoure, quhairvpoun thay caryit him to his said house violentlie and aganis his will and haueing enterit in the house the saidis Johnne Straquhan [and others before named] forcit the said Capitane Alexander to oppin his said chairtour kist in his house of Balfour and deliuer to thame the foirsaid renunciatioun after the resset quhairof They of new agane caryit him bak with thame as captiue and presoner to the said Alexander Straquhan of Thornetoun and than with mony scornefull reproichfull spetchis dimittit him and his servandis quhairby as thay haue vsurpit vpoun thame his maiesteis royall pouer and auctoritie in taking and deteuing of the said Capitane Alexander and his servandis as presoneris sua haue thay violat his maiesteis lawis and actis of parliament maid aganis the convocatioun of his maiesteis leigeis in airmes and beiring and weiring of hagbutis and pistolletis, and with that they haue committit a verie grite insolence vpoun the said complenair in forcing of him with threatning and minassing speitcheis to deliuer his proper euident and write out of his chairter kist within his aue house for the quhilk the saidis personis and ilkane of thame aucht to be persewit and punist in thair personis and goudis . . . And anent the chairge gevin to the said Alexander Straquhane of Thortoun [and the others before named] To haue compeirit personalie [with the exception of the said Robert Irving] before the lordis of sacrite counsall this present fyftene day of September instant . . . Quhilkis being callit and the saidis personnis compeirand personalie . . . The Lordis of secrite counsall assoilzeis simpliciter the saidis defendaris . . . in so far as it concerned the violence done to the said Capitane Alexander Wischart etc. . . . But preiudice alwyse to the said Capitane Alexander Wishart to pursew for deliuerie bak agane to him of the said renunciatioun . . . And siclyke the saidis lordis ordanis lettres to be direct chairging officiaris . . . to pas and deunnce the said Robert Irving who compeirit not his maiesteis rebel and put him to the horne and to eschete etc " (Reg. Sec. Concilii).

In a document contained among the " Acta " of the Privy Council, Alexander Strachan of Thornton and Sir Robert Arbuthnot of that ilk, " neir nichtbouris and kinnismen," are, sometime between 1615 and 1617, on account of " variance and controversie anent the teinding of some lands, they disdaneing the ordinar cours of law and justice, bound to find caution to keep the peace " (Reg. Sec. Sig., vol. 1615-17, fol. 63).

On the 1st August 1616, Alexander Strachan of Thornton obtained ratification of a charter of the lands of Over Craignestown (Privy Seal Register, vol. lxxxiv., fol. 293). He, and the heirs-male of his body, received on the 25th July 1616, a charter of *novodamus* of the lands and barony of Thornton (Privy Seal Register, lxxxiv., fol. 231). On the 9th March 1617, confirmation was given to a lease for nineteen years, granted by the College of Aberdeen, to Alexander Strachan of Thornton, of the teinds of Hauchheid, Mains of Thornton, etc., in the parish of Aberluthnot. The lease describes Mr John Strachan, parson of Kincardine, as rector of the college (Privy Council Records, lxxxvii., fol. 3). On the 14th March 1622, Alexander Strachan of Thornton had confirmation of a charter granted to him by David Tullo of Craignestoun and Jean Strachan, his spouse, and Alexander Tullo, their eldest son, of the barony of Craignestoun, etc. (Reg. Sec. Sig., vol. xci., fol. 373).

On the 17th June 1617, Alexander Strachan of Thornton, Kincardineshire, sat in Parliament along with Sir Robert Graham of Morphie, as representative of Kincardineshire; he was, on the 25th June, appointed a Provisional Commissioner for the Plantation of Churches (Acta Parl. Scot., iv. 525, 531). He was one of three notable persons who were created baronets of Nova Scotia on the 28th May 1625; the two others were Sir Robert Gordon of Letterfourie, son of Alexander, Earl of Sutherland, and William, Earl Marischal (Regist. Precep. Cart. pro Baronettis Nov. Scotiae). Each Nova Scotia baronet paid on his creation 3000 merks, or £166, 13s. 4d. sterling, in return for a nominal grant of 1600 acres in the new colony. On the roll of the Nova Scotia baronets, Sir Alexander Strachan of Thornton ranked next to Gordon of Letterfourie, the premier baronet.

On the 13th April 1626, " Sir Alexander Strachan, knyght baronet," received a royal licence, dated Whitehall, authorising him " to export and cause be exported from hence to our kingdome of Scotland, to his own vse, and the better saiftie and defence of that kingdome, corslettis, pickis, and muskettis, bandelieris, and all armes competent for fourtie pikmen, and so many musketerris, with a reasonable proportion of powder, schot, matches," etc. In 1627, when the Earl of Nithsdale was commissioned by Charles I. to levy three regiments of foot for the service of the King of Denmark (Balfour's Annals), Sir Alexander Strachan drew up a scheme, embracing certain details. To that scheme the attention of Lord Nithsdale was invited in two letters addressed to him by James, Lord Ogilvie, afterwards Earl of Airlie. In the first letter, which is dated Ballashone, 21st June 1627, Lord Ogilvie begs that his correspondent "will move the Lords of the Council 'to distribute all the shyris of this kingdom equalis betwix the colonallis, with the reseruationes and provisiones contined in the paper penned be Thorntoun;' he desires that the Mernes [Kincardineshire] should be assigned to [the laird of] Thorntoun" (Fraser's Book of Carlaverock, vol. ii., pp. 81, 82). On the 7th November 1628, he was commissioned to collect certain rents belonging to his Majesty, omitted from the Exchequer collections, he and his heirs being allowed half of these rents in recompense (Paper Register of the Great Seal, vol. ii., fol. 346). In 1630 he was appointed a Commissioner of Exchequer and a Commissioner for anditing the Treasury accounts. In 1631 he received £3000 for surrendering certain of his commissions to the Crown. In 1633 he witnessed the resignation by William, Earl of Angus, of his hereditary right of the first seat and vote in Parliament (Acta Parl., v. 10). He was in 1635 one of the jurors at the trial of Lord Balmerino, indicted for having in his possession an illegal petition addressed to the king.

Sir Alexander Strachan became deeply embarrassed. On the 13th November 1623, a charter was confirmed, by which Sir Alexander granted to John Wood, merchant-burgess of Edinburgh, the Mains of Craignestown (Reg. Sec. Sig., vol. xciv., fol. 19). In August 1626, Sir Alexander granted a bond for 3000 merks Scots to Laurence Henrysone, merchant-burgess of Edinburgh, in behalf of Mause and Rebecca Henrysone, his dochters. To this instrument, John Strachan, younger of Thornton, and John Strachan of Goislie, are cautioners, while "Mr John and Thomas Strachan," described as "servitors to the said Sir Alexander Strachan," are subscribing witnesses (Register of Deeds, vol. 512). To his relative, James Strachan of Fettercairn, burgess of Edinburgh, he disposed of certain lands at Kincardine in 1628 (see *postea*). On the 18th April 1634, he granted a bond to John Wood of Craigniston for £3166, 6s. 8d., "borrowed money," the cautioners being "John Strachan in Glenfarquhare," described as the granter's uncle, Mr John Strachan of Muretoun, Robert Middeltoun of Caddon, and Alexander Strachan of Goislie. Among the witnesses are "Thomas Strachan, brother to Mr John Strachan, in Glenfarquhar," and "John Strachan, son to the tutor of Thorntoun" (Register of Deeds, vol. 512). To Lady Marion Douglas (Lady Drum), Sir Alexander granted, on the 27th October 1638, an obligation for 1080 merks (Register of Deeds, vol. 569). On the 17th December 1638, John Kennedy of Argeycht obtained a charter of the barony of Thornton, apprised from Sir Alexander Strachan for a debt of 9596 merks (Privy Seal Register). James Strachan of Fettercairn received, on the 2d September 1641, a charter of the lands of Easter and Wester Arnbarrow, in the shire of Kincardine, also apprised from Sir Alexander Strachan, by decreet dated 4th September 1638, for a debt of 8868 merks (Privy Seal Register, vol. cx., fol. 109). Sir Alexander died before 1643.

Sir Alexander Strachan, the first baronet, was twice married. His first wife was Margaret, third daughter of John Lindsay of Balcarres, second son of Sir David Lindsay of Glenesk, and grandfather of Alexander, first Earl of Balcarres. The contract of marriage, dated at "the kirk of Stracathro, 19th January 1605," is subjoined:

"It is agreed and finally contracted betwixt Sir David Lyndsay of Edzell, knight, one of the senators of the College of Justice, for himself, and taking the burden on him for Margaret Lyndsay, lawful daughter to umquhill Mr John Lyndsay of Balcarres, secretary to the King, and the said Margaret for herself as principal, and William Blair of Balgillo, William Maull, burgess of Edinburgh, and Mr James Donaldsoun, advocate, as cautioners and sureties for the said Sir David, on the one part; and Alexander Strathauchin of Thorntoun, with the special advice and consent of his curators, that the said Alexander Strathauchin shall marry the said Margaret Lyndsay, and the said Margaret shall likewise take the said Alexander for her lawful husband, in face of holy kirk; and the said Alexander obliges him, his heirs and assignees, to duly and sufficiently infeft the said Margaret in liferent during all the days of her lifetime in all and haill the town and lands of Pitgarve, the town and lands of Burgatoun, the half Milntoun of Thornetoun, with the third of the corn-mill of Thornetoun, third mill land, multures, etc., thereof, the Browstar Stat land of Thornetoun, the walkmill of Thornetoun and walkmill lands, all which lands are alienated to certain persons under reversions, containing in all the sum of 10,000 merks; and also shall infeft her in liferent in   acres of land of his lands of Kyncardin, the town and lands of Caldhame, the two parts of the mill and mill-lands aforesaid of Thornetoun, or in any other lands of the barony of Thornetoun which the said Sir David Lyndsay and curators to the said Alexander Strathauchin shall think meet; and that by double infeftments they are to be held of the said Alexander Strathauchin and his heirs in fee for one pound yearly, to be paid at Whitsunday, if asked for—the other infeftment to be held of the said Alexander's immediate superiors: And he further obliges him to redeem to the said Margaret with the sums of tocher after mentioned, before Whitsunday next to come, as much of the said lands as shall pay 260 bolls yearly; the said Margaret to have entry to the possession of as much of the remanent of the liferent as shall pay 124 bolls victual, thereby completing to her in liferent 24 chalders victual at the decease of the first of the liferenters of the lands and barony of Thorntoun, and that in contentation of all terce, etc., she may crave of the lands of Thorntoun; for which causes the said Sir David and his afore-mentioned cautioners engage to pay to the said Alexander, etc., the sum of 13,000 merks before Whitsunday next to come, to be employed for the redemption of as much of the said lands as shall pay 260 bolls victual; and for the said tocher the said Margaret shall assign to David Lyndsay of Balcarres, her brother, all goods and gear pertaining to her by the decease of John Lyndsay of Balcarres, her father, Marion Guthrie, her mother, and John Lyndsay of Balcarres, her eldest brother, and shall renounce that part of the lands of Eister Pittorthie in which she was infeft under reversion of 2000 merks.

"Subscribed by David Lyndsay of Edzell, Williame Blair of Balgillo, cautioner, Alexander Strathauchin of Thornetoun, Margaret Lyndesay, J. Levingstoun of Donypace, curator, Mr Johne Strathauchin, curator, J. Strathauchane of Monboddow, curator, Johne Strathauchin, curator, Al. Brechin, witness, Alexander Stratoun of that ilk, witness, Paull Fraser, witness. Dated at the Kirk of Stracathrow, 19th January 1605."

"Registered in the Books of Counsel, 9th July 1608, at the instance of Sir David Lyndsay of Edzell, knight, William Blair of Balgillo, and Margaret Lyndsay, on the one part; and Alexander Strathauchin of Thorntoun, John Levingstoun of Donypace, Mr John

Strathauchin, Mr James Strathauchin of Monboddow, and John Strathauchin, his uncle, on the other part" (Register of Deeds, vol. 149, fol. 326).

Sir Alexander married, secondly, Margaret, widow of George, fifth Earl Marischal, and daughter of James, sixth Lord Ogilvie (Privy Seal Register, vol. cvi., fol. 397, and Withie's Pedigrees). In the Justiciary Records, under the year 1624, are set forth certain proceedings connected with a criminal charge preferred against Sir Alexander Strachan of Thornton, and Dr Robert Strachan, for the forcible seizure of articles of jewellery and silver plate, "at the place of Benholme," belonging to the late George, Earl Marischal. The articles stolen are enumerated as:

"Of Portugal ducats and other species of foreign gold, to the avail of twenty thousand pounds or thereby; thretty-sax dozen of gold buttons; ane rich jewel all set with diamonts, whilk the earl resavit as ane gift given to him, the time he was ambassador in Denmark, worth sax thousand merks; the Queen of Denmark's picture in gold, set about with rich diamonts, estimat to five thousand merks; ane jasp staue for steming of bluid, estimat to five hundred French crowns; ane chenyie of equal pearl, wherein was four hundred pearls great and small; twa chenyies of gold, of twenty-four unce weeht; ane other jewel of diamonts set in gold, worth three hundred merks; ane great pair of bracelets, all set with diamonts, price thereof five hundred crowns; the other pair of gold bracelets at sax hundred pounds the pair; ane turcas ring, worth ten French crowns; ane diamont set in ane ring, price twenty-eight French crowns; with ane number of other small rings set with diamonts and other rich stanes in gold, worth three hundred French crowns; mair sixteen thousand merks of silver and gold ready-cunyit, whilk was within the said green coffer; together with the haill tapestry, silver-work, bedding, and other guids, geir, and plenishing, being within the said place."

In the criminal charge James Keith of Benholm, and the Countess Marischal, wife of Sir Alexander Strachan, were included. Some of the proceedings on the trial are subjoined:

"Curia Justiciarie, S. D. N. Regis tenta pretorio de Edinburgh, Tertio Martii 1624, per dominium Georgium Erskine de Innerteill Justiciarium.

"Intrantes—Sir Alex^{r.} Strauchine of Thornetoun, knt., Mr Robert Strauchine, doctour in Phisik.

"Dilaittit of the maisterfull thift and stouthereiff ffurth of the place of Benholme, perteining to vmquhile George, erle Merschell, of certaine his lordschippis jowellis, siluer plait, houshald stuff, gold, siluer, and euidentis perteining to the said erle of Merschell, . . . as expressed at lenth in the criminal letters directed thereupon, committit in October 1622, a littill befoir the said erles deceis. Persavaris Sir William Oliphaut of Newton, his Majesteis aduocat. Prelocutouris in defence, Mr Thomas Hoip, Mr Lewis Stewart.

"A warrand from the counsall was presented to the justice, for continewing the dyet to the 2 July next to come, warrand dated Edr. 2 Mar. 1624. The warrand states that the lords of Secrit Counsall, for some special considerations moving them, ordains to continue the action appointed to Dame Margaret Ogilvie, Countess of Merschell, Sir Alexr. Strauchane of Thornetoun, hir spous, and vtheris persones specifeit in the criminal letteris, taking new caution for their compearance. Sir George Affleck of Balmanno, knight, becomes security for the Countess, Sir Alexander Strauchane, and Mr Rot. Strauchane, doctour in phisick. On the 2 July 1624, the pannell presented ane warrand of the lords of Secreit Counsall direct to the justice, commanding him to continew the dyet appointed to the laird of Thorntoun, the Lady Merschell, hir spous, the laird of Benholme, and Dr Strauchane, to xxvij July instant, upon new caution, and to dispens with the personal compearance of the Lady Merschell, and Doctour Strauchane. Dated Halyruidhous, 1 July 1624. On the 27th July 1624, the pannell produced the counsells warrand for continewing of this matter, and all tryell to be tane thairintill to the aucht day of December nixt. The warrand gives the names, Dame Margaret Ogilvy, Lady Merschell, the Laird of Thornetoun, hir husband, and Mr Robert Strauchane, doctour in phisick. Dated Halyruidhous, 22 July 1624. Dauid Levingstoune of Donypace, becomes cautioner."

In a letter to the Chancellor Hay, dated 22d August 1624, King James, alluding to a recommendation he had formerly sent, suggesting that the injury to the Earl Marischal should be inquired into, adds, "It was not our pleasure nor meaning to hurt the said Lady Marischal, or any other person; these are now expressly to mak it known to you, that we nather gave direction to insert any sic clause in our letters, nather at the putting of our hand to the samen, did tak heed thereto, nor never meant any sic favour to her who hath so ill deserved of one, for whose sake we were only to respect her." The king further ordered the case to be proceeded with (Analecta Scotica).

The dispute was amicably adjusted, as would appear from the following remission under the Privy Seal, dated at Whitehall, 13th April 1626:

"His Majesty, and the Commissioners for granting remissions, etc., understanding that before the decease of the late George, Earl Marischal, father of William, now Earl Marischal, various controversies arose between the said Earl George, William and Lady Margaret Ogilvie, spouse of the said Earl George, and James Keith of Benhame, eldest son of the said Earl George and Margaret, his lady, especially about the moveable goods pertaining to the said late Earl; and the said Lady Margaret; James Keith, her son; Sir Alexander Strachan of Thornton, Kt.; Sir William Douglas of Glenbervie, Kt.: Mr Robert Strachan, Doctor of Medicine, and others, 'fraudi criminis socii et assistentes,' stole and carried off certain chests, writings, evidence, gems, gold, silver, etc., from the mansions of Benhame and Fetteresso, and other places, as seemed best to the said Lady Margaret and James Keith, for their security; which act of spoliation is hereby remitted by confirmation of a contract containing clause of exoneration of the same between the said parties" (Reg. Sec. Sig., vol. xcix., fol. 87).

Sir Alexander Strachan of Thornton, second baronet of Thornton, and Colonel John Keith, brother of William, Earl Marischal, were, on the 22d March 1652, joint-borrowers of 400 merks from Alexander Innes, merchant in Edinburgh (Register of Deeds, vol. 603).

By his first marriage, Sir Alexander Strachan had two sons, John and Alexander. The name of the former occurs as "fiar of Thornton," in an obligation granted by Sir Alexander, in August 1626, to Laurence Henrysone (see *supra*); he must have died prior to the 1st August 1635, the date of the subjoined charter, in which Alexander Strachan is described as "only lawful son of Sir Alexander Strachan." This charter, granted by Charles I., is dated 1st August 1635. It confirms

"A charter of infeftment and precept of sasine by Sir Alexander Strauchane, knight baronet, described as 'his Majesty's counsellor,' to Alexander Strauchane, only lawful son of the said Sir Alexander, and to Elizabeth Douglas, his spouse, and the longest liver of them in conjunct fee, and to their heirs-male; whom failing, to the heirs-male of the body of the said Alexander; whom failing, to the heirs-male and assignees whatsoever of the said Sir Alexander Strauchane of Thornetoun, knight: Of all and whole that part of the Mains of Thornetoun called the Meynes of Thornetoun, the town and lands of Burgartoun, the town and third of the Mylnetoun of Thornetoun, with the mill of the same as therein specified, the town and lands of Brigtoun, with the whole of that part of the Mains of Thornetoun called the Hanchheid of Thornetoun, in special warrandice of the foresaid lands of Brigtoun, with the houses and other pertinents of the said lands lying in the barony of Thornetoun, in the parish of Abirluthnot and shire of Kincardine: and it is provided that, should the said Elizabeth Douglas be interfered with in the peaceful possession of the said town and lands of Brigtoun by Lady Margaret Ogilvie, spouse of the said Sir Alexander, by virtue of any claim she had to the same, then the said Elizabeth was to have free access to the said Hauchheid of Thornetoun till she should be able to enjoy peaceably the lands of Brigtoun—the manor place of Thornetoun; also of the old park or grove, the park of Thornetoun lying on the east side of the Loning, which divides the old park from other two new parks; the Cairberzaird, lying to the south and east of the said old park; the seven and a half acres or thereabouts lying on the east side of the plantation of Thornetoun, which were formerly parts of the lands of Bent, and disponed to the said Sir Alexander Strauchane by Sir Alexander Falconer of Halkertoun; that eastern part of the marsh of Bent, which was also disposed to the former by the latter, with the privilege and perpetual servitude of one cairtgait, of the breadth of sixteen feet or thereabouts, for the transportation of the 'glebae' of the said Sir Alexander Strauchane, from the said marsh to the dwelling-house of Thornetoun, through that part of the marsh and lands pertaining to the said Sir Alexander Falconer: Reserving to the said Sir Alexander Strauchane his liferent of the manor-place of Thornetoun, with the tower, fortalice, etc., thereof, together with the old park of Thornetoun, and the charterzaird and the seven and a half acres lying on the east side of the plantation of Thornetoun as aforesaid, and the foresaid privilege of the cairtgait, in manner and effect as is more fully stated in the contract in which the charter proceeds: To be held of the Crown, the immediate superiors of the said Sir Alexander, by him and his heirs in fee and heritage for ever, under the provisions, conditions, etc., specified in the said contract and charter: Reserving to the Crown, besides, etc." (Reg. Sec. Sig., cvi., fol. 397).

On the 19th January 1650, Sir Alexander Strachan, second baronet of Thornton, granted an obligation to John Mophet, elder, merchant-burgess of Edinburgh, for £500 Scots, borrowed money. The subscription is witnessed by Harrie Strauchan, cousing (cousin), and John Strachan, servitor to the said Sir Alexander (Register of Deeds, vol. 587).

The subsequent history of the second baronet is imperfectly known. Having become dispossessed of his estates, he latterly retreated to Flanders (Acta Parl. Scot., vi. 586-595). He died at Bruges in 1659. His testament-dative and inventory, given up by David Strachan,[1] merchant-burgess of Edinburgh, are of the following tenor:

[1] " Vigesimo septimo Julij j^m vj^e quinquagesimo nono (1659).
"The same day in pns forsaid Dauid Strauchin, mertchant, compeirand, is made Burges and gildbrother of this burgh, as prenteis to Johne Meyne, merchant, burges and gildbrother thereof, and hes givin his oath in maner abonewrittin, and payed for his dewtie to the dean of gild—xv lib." (Guild Register of Edinburgh, vol. iii.).

"The Testament dative and Inventar of the goods, gear, sums of money, and debts, of umquhill Sir Alexander Strauchane of Thornetoune, who died at Brudges, in West Flanders, in the month of —— 1659 years, faithfully made and givne up be David Strauchane, merchant-burges of Edinburgh, only executor dative for himself and as assigned wnderwrittin, only executor dative decerned as creditor to him in swa far as the said vmquhill Sir Alexander Strauchane be his Ticket or missive lettrewill writtin and subscryved with his awine hand of the daitt the xv day of May 1657 zeirs mentioning whereas the said vmquhill defunct had receaved ten old peices of the said David his money. Thairfor giving him warrand to receave his twa coller cloathes from Williame Strauchane in Inchgray with the velvett pock and keip them in suretie for his money for the quhich he was to pay annual rent at the redemptione of the foirsaid goodes . . . and siclyk the said Sir Alexander be his Ticket . . . of the daitt the xij day of February 1658 zeers granted him to be . . . restand awand to the said David Strachane the sowme of xiij^c. xlvj^{lib.} iiij^{s.} vsuall scottes money . . . and in lyk manner the said vmquhill Sir Alexander Strauchane be ane Bill of Exchange drawne be him on the said David Strachane . . . of the daitt the threttie day of October 1658 zeiris did thairby ordour the said David Strauchane . . . to pay . . . to Mr Gilbert Thomsone . . . iiij^cl. gilders ellevine stivers and ane half . . . for reddic money lent . . . as the said Bill of the daitt foirsaid (quhich is all of the Dutch languadge) . . . at mair lenth couteines. He [the said Sir Alexander] be his assignatione . . . of the daitt the second day of February 1660 . . . maid and constitute the said David Strauchane his undoubted cessioner and assignay . . . and that be decreit of the commissaris of Edinburgh . . . of the daitt the day of October 1661 zeiris . . .

"Therefore the said David is only executor-dative to the said Sir Alexander, and decerned creditor for the sums above specified, that is, the ten old pieces, the sum of £1346, 4s. Scots, and the sum 450 guilders 11½ stivers, Flemish money, at 22s. Scots the guilder, the whole extending to £496, 12s. Scots; and for the annual rent of the ten old pieces; and for the expenses of confirmation of the present testament, in so far as the said umquhill Sir Alexander's goods will extend to, and may be recovered; and that by decreet of the Commissioners of Edinburgh, dated — October 1661.

"Availis pertaining to Sir Alexander at his decease, viz.: 'Thrie old trunks containing thairintill iii^c xxxvi old books, estimat all to lxxij lib. Scottes money; Item, ane bloodstone, valued to the sowme of iii^c lib. Scottes money foirsaid; Item, ane eglis stone, valued to i^c lib. money foirsaid; Item, ane spleane stone, worth l lib.; Item, fyve or sax nauchtie stones, worth iiii Scottes money; Item, ane reid skierlett coat, with lace thereon, worth xx lib.; Item, ane coller cloath with bag, estimat to i^c lib.; Item, ane hagbitt or gun, worth xii lib.; Item, certane uther plennisching belonging to the defunct, estimat all *in cumulo* to the sowme of ii^c lib. Scottes money above writtin.

"Summa of Inveuter, viii^c lviii lib." (Edin. Com. Reg., vol. lxx.).

David Strauchane, skinner-burgess of Edinburgh, is cautioner.

The following charter of resignation to Thomas Allardyce, tutor of

Allardyce of the lands of Haucheid, and others, relates to lands possessed by the deceased baronet :

"Oliver be the grace of God, lord protector of the commonwealth of Ingland Scotland Ireland and dominions therevnto belonging . . . give grant and dispone . . . to Thomas Allardes tutor of Ardes his heirs and assigneyes whatsomever heritably . . . All and sindry thes pairtes and portiones of the lands and barony of Thornetoun aftermentionat. To witt all and haill the landes of Haucheid except such pairts and portiones thereof as wer formerlie disponed be Sir Alexander Strauchane of Thornetoun Knight Baronet and the deceist John Strauchane of Haucheid To Sir Frances Ogilvie of New Grange and which are presently possest be George Mathie John Gentleman and James Ros, Midmaynes of Thornetoun, toune and lands of Brigtonne etc. . . . with tour fortalice and manor place of Thornetoun . . . all lying within the barony of Thorntoun, parish of Abirluthnot and schirefdom of Kincardin—which lands &c. pertained heritably to Sir Alexander Strauchane of Thornetouue Alexander Strauchane elder of Glenkindie the said deceast John Strauchane of Haucheid and John Kennedy of Cairnmuckes held of us in place of the last king ; and the said haill lands and barony were resigned by the said John Kennedy by his procurators at Edinburgh for new infeftment to have been made under the great seal to the said Sir Alexander Strauchane of Thornetoune as assigney his aires &c. in virtue of a procuratorie of resignation made by the said John Kennedy resigning the said haill lands and barony in the hands of the Commissioners of Exchequer in favour of the deceast Master James Strauchane sometime of Fetterkairne his aires and assigneyes and exprest in the disposition made be the said deceist Master James of the dait the 20 January 1644, registered in the books of Council and Session 15 June 1646 and conforme to the assignation and disposition thereof made by the said deceist Maister James to the said Sir Alexander Strauchane his aires and assigneyes of the date 12 April 1648 registered in books aforesaid 17 April same year. Which premisses so far as concerns the parts and portions abovementioned of the foresaid baronie of Thornetoune disponed to the said Thomas Allardes were assigned and disponed be the said Alexander Strauchane elder of Glenkindie Sir Alexander and John Strauchanes to the said Thomas Allardes his heirs and assigneyes heritably by disposition dated 3 January last by past and as the disposition assignation &c. made be the said Sir Alexander Strauchane to the said Thomas Allardes dated . . . declares :

"And the parts portions &c. above rehersed as so disponed were resigned be the said Sir Alexander Strauchane, Alexander Strauchane elder of Glenkindie and the deceist John Strauchane of Haucheid at Edinburgh for new infeftment to be made to the said Thomas Allardes & his heirs &c. heritably according to disposition thereof made to him by the said Alexander Strauchane elder of Glenkindie with consent of the said Sir Alexander Strauchane and John Strauchane dated 3 January last by past."

The charter contains precept of sasine, and is dated at Edinburgh, 3d July 1657 (Reg. Mag. Sig., lib. lix. 47).

Sir Alexander Strachan, second baronet of Thornton, died without issue. From the will of Alexander Strachan of Thornton, dated 14th May 1601, it appears that at the death of that person, which took place the same month, his male descendants were Alexander Strachan, only child of Robert, his eldest son, deceased, afterwards the first baronet, and father of Alexander, the second baronet; John, his second son, and one of his executors; and George, his third son, who was a witness to his will.

George Strachan, described as "father's brother" to Alexander Strachan of Thornton, received, on the 14th December 1613, a gift of the "escheat of John Young in Laurenstoun at the horn" (Privy Seal Register). He resided in "Cottoun of Inglistoun, in the parish of Kinnettles, and county of Forfar, and there died, unmarried, in April 1626, his affairs being administered by his brother-german, John Strachan" (Commissariat Register of St Andrews, vol. iii., December 15, 1626).

John Strachan, second son of Alexander Strachan of Thornton, obtained, on the 17th December 1601, "a gift of the escheat of his father, the late Alexander Strachan of Thornton," who was put to the horn for debt at the instance of Alexander Elphinstone, son of Alexander, Master of Elphinstone (Privy Seal Register, vol. lxxi., fol. 371). On the 24th December 1602, he got a suspension against Alexander Elphinstone, son of Alexander, Master of Elphinstone, who had denounced as rebel, for non-payment of certain sums of money, " the said late Alexander Strachan," and had, by raising letters of treason, sought to possess himself of " the place of Thornetoun ;" the keys of Thornton House were delivered to Sir George Home of Spot, Treasurer of the Kingdom (Privy Seal Register, vol. 1601-2, fol. 757).

On the 14th March 1622, John Strachan, then residing at Phesdo, and Isabel Rait, his spouse, received confirmation, in conjunct fee, of the lands of Phesdo and Broadlands, in the parish of Fordoun, without prejudice to the possession by Sir Alexander Strachan of the whole other lands and barony of Thornton, in terms of a contract between him and John Strachan, dated 29th September 1618 (Privy Seal Register, vol. xci. 376). On the 7th March 1628, a charter by Sir Alexander Strachan of Thornton was confirmed, granting to John Strachan the lands of Goislie, in the thanage of Fettercairn and parish of Marykirk (Privy Seal Register, vol. c., fol. 340). As "John Strachan of Goislie," he is one of the cautioners of Sir Alexander Strachan, in his bond for 3000 merks to Laurence Henrysone (see *supra*). In a disposition by Sir Alexander Strachan, Bart., dated 19th July 1628, in favour of James Strachan of Fettercairn, burgess of Edinburgh, of portions of the lands of Kincardine, the instrument bears that it is executed "with consent of John Strachan his uncle, and Mr Robert Strachan, doctor of physic" (General Register of Deeds, vol. ccccxix., 13th July 1629).

In 1643, John Strachan is designated "tutor of Thornton," and in March 1647, he is described as "John Strachan of Hauchheid" (Acta Parl. Scot., vol. vi., p. 280). As John Strachan of Haughheid, he, on the 18th July 1653, granted a disposition to Robert Burnett of Elvick of the town and lands of Little Colpnay, and the town and lands of Greendew, in the parish of Belhelvie and county of Aberdeen (Reg. of Deeds, vol. 610). He married, first, Isabel Rait, and, secondly, Margaret Wood. He seems to have had two sons. John Strachann, "son of the tutor of Thornton," is named in the bond granted by Alexander Strachan to John Wood in April 1634, and in same instrument is named "Alexander Strauchan of Goislie," who may fairly be presumed to have received that property on the surrender of his father, who had a charter to the lands of Goislie, and was formerly designed of that place. Both sons would appear to have predeceased their father, for in a bond dated 30th November 1661, and granted by Sir James Strachan of Thornton, to Margaret Wood, widow of "John Strachan of Hauchheid, for 2000 merks," the granter names as their children four daughters, Elizabeth, Katherine, Isobel, and Margaret Strachan (General Register of Deeds, vol. xii.). John Strachan, variously styled of Phesdo, Goislie, and Hauchheid, and "tutor of Thornton," died prior to the 3d July 1657, for in a charter of the lands of Hauchheid of that date, he is named as "the decesit John Strachan of Hauchheid " (Reg. Mag. Sig., lib. lix., No. 47).

The direct male line of Alexander Strachan of Thornton, grandfather of Sir Alexander Strachan, the first baronet, became extinct on the death of Sir Alexander, the second baronet, in 1659. The patent of baronetcy granted to the first baronet on the 28th May 1625, bore that the dignity was conferred on him and his heirs-male, " suisque heredibus masculis in perpetuum" (Playfair's Baronetage, vol. iii., Appendix, p. 170). The third baronet, we shall find, was descended from a remote ancestor of the first baronet.

William Strachan of Monboddo, third son of John Strachan of Thornton, great-great-granduncle of the first baronet, obtained the honour of knighthood. He married Margaret, daughter of Sir James Ramsay of Balmain, and had issue, a son, James, and a daughter, Jean.

Jean, daughter of Sir William Strachan of Monboddo, married Sir John Orchardton of Orchardton, parish of Udny, Aberdeenshire, as is attested in the following birth-brief, dated at Edinburgh, 6th August 1663 :

"CAROLUS, etc.—Quum ergo dilectus noster subditus dominus Joannes Orchardtounus in exercitum sub auspiciis serenissimi Suedorum regis vigilum prefectus supplex a nobis postulasset vt que de ipsius natalibus et prosapia vel hominum memoria vel antiquissimis regni Scotie monumentis constarent publico nostro diplomate testata faceremus, Nos tam honeste petitioni fauentes opera et fide Gulielmi comitis de Glencarne nostri in regno Scotie Cancellarii tota re explorata de ipsius natalibus et majoribus hoc publicum testimonium deserimus. Natus est antedictus dominus Joannes Orchardtoune vigilum prefectus ex legitimo matrimonii thoro parentibus et majoribus vtrinque in hoc regno nobilitate et virtute primariis patre domino Andrea Orchardtoune Orchardtounii Comarcho in vicecomitatu nostro Abredonensi matre domina Elisebetha Robertsona illius conjuge legitima fuit autem Andreas Orchardtounus, Orchardtounii Comarchus filius legitimus domini Joannes Orchardtouni, Orchardtounii Comarchi ex illius conjuge Elisabetha Auchinlecka que filia fuit legitima domini Georgii Auchinlecki Pitrichie ex antiquissima Balmanie baronum familia oriundi in vicecomitatu nostro Perthensi baronis in suprema Scotorum curia Senatoris amplissimi ex illius conjuge domina Anna Raita domini Jacobi Raiti Halgreene baronis filia legitima. Et hic quoque dominus Joannes Orchardtoune Orchardtounii Comarchus domini Joannis Orchardtounii, vigilinm prefecti avus filius fuit legitimus domini Jacobi Orchardtouni, Orchardtounii Comarchi ex domina Joanna Strachana, parentes habuit dominum Guliclmum Strachaun Monboddc Comarchum ex antiquissima Strachanorum Thorntounii baronum in vicecomitatu nostro Kincardiensi familia recta linea oriundum opibus honore potentia et avita rerum gestarum gloria imprimis refulgente" (Reg. Mag. Sig., Com. Carta Affret, lib. v., vi., fol. 137).

Translated into English the birth-brief proceeds thus:

"CHARLES.—Since, therefore, our well-beloved subject, Sir John Orchardton, captain of the guards in the army of his Serene Highness the King of Sweden, has asked and petitioned us to make a diploma certified by public testimony as to what is known of his birth and lineage, either from memory of man, or the most ancient records of the kingdom of Scotland; we being well inclined to so honourable a petition, and a search having been made into the whole matter, by the assistance and fidelity of William, Earl of Glencairn, Chancellor of our kingdom, give this public testimonial regarding his birth and ancestry. The foresaid Sir John Orchardton, captain of the guards, was born in lawful wedlock of parents and ancestors on both sides in the first rank for nobility and worth in this kingdom—his father being Sir Andrew Orchardtoune, laird of Orchardtoune in the sheriffdom of Aberdeen, his mother Lady Elizabeth Robertson, the latter's lawful spouse. And Andrew Orchardtoun, laird of Orchardtoun, was lawful son of Sir John Orchardtoun, laird of Orchardtoun, by his spouse, Elizabeth Auchinleck, who was lawful daughter to Sir John Auchinleck of Pitrichie, knight, descended of the very ancient family of the barons of Balmain, in the sheriffdom of Perth, a very distinguished senator in the Supreme Court of Scotland, by his spouse, Lady Anna Rait, lawful daughter of Sir James Rait of Hallgreen, knight. Also this Sir John Orchardtoun, laird of Orchardtoun, grandfather of Sir John Orchardtoun, captain of the guards, was lawful son to Sir James Orchardtoun, laird of Orchardtoun, by Lady Jean Strachan, whose father was Sir William Strachan, laird of Monboddo, descended in a direct line of the most ancient family of the Strachans, barons of Thorntoun, in the shire of Kincardine, especially eminent for wealth, honour, power, and ancestral glory."

To James Strachan of Monboddo (son of Sir William Strachan),

David Beaton, commendator of Arbroath, the future cardinal, on the 10th May 1525, directed a precept for infefting John Wishart of Pitarrow in the mill and lands of Couveth, Kincardineshire (Fraser's Earls of Southesk, p. lxv.). James Strathauchin of Monboddo received a charter from James V., under the Great Seal, dated "Dundee, 20th February 1526." In this charter, "the whole third part of the lands of Arbirny and the lands of Craghall, and Kirkheuch, in the shire of Kincardine, which formerly pertained hereditarily to the said James, and were by him resigned into the king's hands," were granted to him and "Janet Gardin, his spouse, and the longest liver of them in conjunct fee, and to the heirs of the said James" (Reg. Mag. Sig., lib. xxi., 15). John Strachan of Monboddo was, on the 24th July 1548, a witness to the confirmation of a charter in favour of John Strachan of Thornton, by John Strachan of Lenturk (Reg. Mag. Sig., 30, No. 205). On the 8th May 1551, John Strachan of Monboddo received a gift of the ward and non-entry of the lands of Craigyhill, Kincardineshire, on the renunciation thereof by Janet Gardyn, his mother (Reg. Mag. Sig., lib. xxii., fol. 81; Reg. Sec. Sig., vol. xxiv., fol. 81b). On the 4th December 1571, "John Strathauchin of Monbodo," with others, was "delatit for remaining fra the Raid of Leith" (Curia Justiciarie, S.D.N. Regis, 5 Jac. vi.). James Strachan of Monboddo witnessed, on the 15th December 1586, the confirmation of a charter, by Alexander Strachan of Thornton to Robert Strachan, of the lands of Caldome (Reg. Mag. Sig., lib. xxxvi., No. 315). On the 4th January 1591-2, licence was granted to James Strachan of Monboddo, to remain at home on account of his infirmity (Reg. Mag. Sig., lib. lxiii., fol. 108). "James Strauchin of Monbodo" is in the will of Alexander Strachan of Thornton, dated 14th May 1601, mentioned as indebted to the deceased for the year's payment of the feus of Fettercairn and Fordoun (see *supra*).

At the Kirk of Stracathro, on the 13th January 1605, James Strachan of Monboddo subscribed, as one of his curators, the marriage-contract of Alexander, afterwards Sir Alexander Strachan, first baronet of Thornton (Register of Deeds, vol. cxlix., fol. 320).

James Strachan of Monboddo died on the 10th July 1614. The will proceeds thus :—

"*The Testament* testamentar and Inventarie of the gudis, geir, and dettis of umquhill James Strachauchin of Monboddo, within the parochin of Fordoun and Sherefdome of Kincardin, the tyme of his deceis, quha deceissit vpoun the tent day of July 1614 zeiris : ffaythfullie maid and gevin vp be Robert and Dauid Strachauchin, laufull sones to the defunct & executonris testamentaris nominat be him in his Lettre will underwrittin of the dait at Montrois the xxiiij day of September 1612 zeiris.

"In the first, the said umquhill James the tyme of his deceis foirsaid had the guidis and geir following of the prices eftir specifeit viz. of reddie money jᵐ jᶜ lxxxvij lib. vis. viiid.; Item, in vtencillis & domicellis estimat to lxvj lib. xijs. iiijd.

"*Summa* of the Inventarie jᵐ ijᶜ lxiiij lib.

"Dettes awand to the Deid.

"Item, be Robert Lichtoun of Ulyhevin vjᶜ lxvj lib. xijs. iiijd.
"Item, be Robert Grahame of Fernyflet vjᶜ lxvj lib. xijs. iiijd. borrowit money.

"*Summa* of the Dettes—jᵐ iijᶜ xxxiij lib. vjs. viijd.

"Summa of the Inventar and Dettes—ijᵐ vjᶜ lxxxxvij lib. vijs. viijd.

"Quot. by compositioun) To be devydit in tua partes : ilk part is jᵐ ijᶜ xxxxviij lib. xlviij lib. xijs. vjd.) xiijs. iiijd.

"ffollowis the Lattir will.

"At Montrois the xxiiij day of September the zeir of God jᵐ vjᶜ tuelf zeiris. I, James Strachauhin of Monboddo being haill in bodie, God be prasit, makis my testament and lettre will in maner and forme following. To wit, in the first I leave and committis my saull to the eternall god, the creator thairof, & to Jesus Chryst his onlie sone and the holie gost the redemer and conservatour of the samyn ; my bodie to the erth to be honnestlie buriet amangis the faythfull in ane Christian buriele, quhen and quhair God pleissis thair to rest vnto the day of God's generall judgement in houp and assurance of the resurrection to everlasting Lyf baith of bodie and saull in the heavins with our saviour Chryst and his angillis. And be thir presentes, makis, nominates, constitutes and ordaines my verie assured & weilbelouittis Robert and Dauid Strachauchinis my sones, my onlie executoures testamentaris & intromitteres with my haill guidis and geir efter my deceis and thai to pay faythfullie as thai will answer to God my haill dettis and legaceis and that be the sicht counsall and advyce of Mr Andro Arbuthnot of Little Sutheis my sone in law, quhom be ther presentes I nominat ovirsman to my saidis executoures, and leavis to him & his bairnes my oyis the sowme of sex hundreth merkis. In witnes heirof I have written & subscryuit thes presentes with my hand, day zeir and place foirsaidis; befoir thir witnessis Mr Andro Strachauchin minister at Dun; Mr Thomas Burnet minister at the kirk of Strachauchin; James Tullo, my seruand

(sic subscribitur)   J. STRACHAUCHIN of Monbuddo.

Mr Thomas Burnet, witnes; James Tulloch, witnes; Mr Andro Strachauchin, witnes. This present Inventarie and Testament befoir written togither with the executoures thairin constitut is confirmat vpoun the xx day of April 1615 zeiris; The saidis executoures maid fayth etc. and Dauid Ramsay zounger of Balman is becum cautioun etc." (Com. Reg. of St Andrews, vol. v., July 5, 1613).

In the preceding will, which is witnessed by Mr Andrew Strachan, minister at Dun (grandson of John Strachan, proprietor of Thornton in the reign of James IV.), the testator names his two sons, Robert and David (Com. Reg. of St Andrews, 20th April 1615). His eldest son, whose Christian name does not appear, had predeceased him, for on the 13th November 1616, "James Strauchauchin of Monbodo" obtained infeftment in a tenement at Montrose, as heir to the late James Strachauchin of Monboddo, his "guidschir" (grandfather) — he thereafter resigning the same for new infeftment in favour of "David Strauchauchin, his father's brother" (Montrose Register of Sasines, vol. 1613-1630, fol. 57). This James Strachan of Monboddo, grandson of the former proprietor, was a trader in Edinburgh. Of that city he was admitted a burgess, on the 1st April 1618; in the Guild Register his admission is thus certified: "Primo Aprilis I^m vi^e decimo octavo. The qlk day in presence of David Aikinheid, deyne of gild, and the gild counsell, Mr James Strathauchin merchand Burges flesere, compeirand sufficientlie airmit with ane furnischt corslet. Is maid gildbrother of this burgh, and has giuin his aith in maner abovenritten. And hes payit for his dewtye to the deyne of gild, j^e lib."

Dealing extensively in cattle, James Strachan became opulent. On the 28th December 1626, he received an obligation from Robert, Earl of Nithsdale, for £4093, 6s. 8d. From William Rait of Balmakewan, he received, on 23d November 1636, a bond for 10,000 merks (Register of Deeds). On the 19th July 1628, he acquired from Sir Alexander Strachan of Thornton, portions of the lands of Kincardine (Register of Deeds, vol. ccccxix., 13th July 1629). Subsequent loans to that baronet, amounting to 8868 merks, not being redeemed, he obtained by royal charter of *novodamus*, dated 13th March 1637, the lands of Over Balmakewan and others, in the parish of Marykirk, which had formerly belonged to Sir Alexander (Reg. Mag. Sig., lv. 315). On the 2d September 1641, he had a charter of apprising under the Great Seal, of the lands of Easter and Wester Arnbarrows, being a portion of the lands of Thornton (Reg. Mag. Sig., lib. iv., No. 378, fol. 432). In March 1645, his house in Fettercairn was "brynt" (burnt) by the soldiers of the Marquis of Montrose (Spalding's Memorials, 1624-1645).

On the 29th March 1650,[1] James Strachan of Fettercairn obtained by a contract of alienation the lands and barony of Inchtuthill or Delvine, in the parish of Caputh, Perthshire. This contract was concluded between Sir Patrick Ogilvie, with consent of Patrick, Lord Ogilvie of Deskford, his eldest son, on the one part, and James Strachan for himself, and in name and on behalf of James, afterwards Sir James Strachan, his eldest son, on the other part. Registered in the books of Council and Session, on the 1st March 1651, this contract contains the following clause: "Providing always that albeit the heritable fie of the lands, barony, mylne, and other foresaids be provydit hereby to the said James Strachan, his airs male and assigneys foresaids, yet he and they

[1] In the Cess Roll of the parish of Caputh for 1649, Mr James Strachan of Inchtuthill is recorded as having a valued rent of £2770 Scots.

are and shall be lyable and subject to the implement and fulfilling of the matrimonial contract passed betwixt the said Mr James Strachan, his father, and Mary Ramsay, with consent of umquhil David Ramsay of Balmayne, her father."

James Strachan of Fettercairn, Monboddo, and Inchtuthill, died on the 6th January 1651. His testament dative with inventory is subjoined (Com. Reg. of Perth, vol. i. fol. 248).

"The Testament dative and Inventar of the guidis, gir, and debtes of vmquhile Mr James Strachane of Insche Stuthill, the tyme of his deceiss, who deceissit upon the sext day of j^m vj^c liftie ane yearis, within the paroschin of Caputh, Sherieffdome and Comissariot of Pearth, faithfullie maid and given up be James Strachan his eldest lawfull sone, executour dative decernit to his said vmquhill father, be decreit of the comissaris of Pearth shyre, given and pronuncit thairanent upon the twentie-auncht day of April j^m vj^c liftie thrie yearis, as ane act maid thair anent proportis.

"INVENTAR.

"Imprimis, the said James Strachan gives up that the said vmquhill Mr James Strachan his father, had pertaining to him and in his possession the tyme forsaid of his deceisse, the guidis and geir following, of the availlis and pryces efter mentionat—viz., ane black horse, pryce xxiiij lib. Item, ane mair, pryce xvi lib. Item, ane young mair, staige, pryce thairof xxxiij lib. vis. viijd. Item, six oxin, pryce of the peice xxxiiij lib.; Inde, je xliiij lib. Item, four old oxin, pryce of the peice overhead xx lib.; Inde, lxxx lib. Item, four young oxin, pryce of the peice overhead xxiiij lib.; Inde, lxxxxvi lib. Item, fyftein key, pryce of the peice over head xx lib.; Inde, iijc lib. Item, four young stirkis, pryce of the peice overhead, x lib.; Inde, xl lib. Item, four calves, pryce of the peice vi lib. xiiis. iiijd.; Inde, xxvi lib. xiijs. iiijd. Item, fyftein old zewis, pryce of the peice over head xls.; Inde, xxx lib. Item, twentie Lambis, pryce of the peice xiijs. iiijd.; Inde, xiij lib. vjs. viijd. Item, the encrease of fyve bollis bear sawing, estimate to the fourt curne—Inde, xx bollis,—pryce of the boll, with the fodder, ix lib.; Inde, j^c lxxx lib. Item, the encrease of fourtie sevin bollis oatis sawing estimat the third curen, Inde, j^c xli bollis, price of the boll with the foder, viij lib. vis. viijd.; Inde, j^m j^c lxxv lib. Item, the vticill and domicill of his house, estimat by the airship to j^c l lib.

"Summa Inventar ij^m iij^c lxxix lib.

"DEBTES AWAND TO THE DEAD.

"Imprimis, be George Mackie in Redghill, lxvi lib. of bygane dentie. Item, be James Willie, j^c xlij lib. iis. off bygane dewtie. Item, be David Ambros and Patrick Angus thair, lxxxiij lib. xs. Item, be Alexr. Levage thair, lxxxvij lib. vs. Item, Lawrance Bydie in Maires, Li lib. Item, be Dauid Gib thair, xxiiij lib. Item, be Jhon Eldge thair, xlvij lib. iiijs. Item, be William Flowrie thair, xviij lib. Item, be Jhon Beat thair, xx lib. Item, be Thomas Michie thair, xlvij lib. 6s. 8d. Item, be Jhon Robertson thair, xxi lib. xs. Item, be Janet Darling thair, xxxi lib. 13s. iiijd. Item, be Jhon Cowper thair, 20 lib. Item, be William Turnbull thair, Lxxx lib. xiijs. iiijd. Item, be Walter Ravery thair, xxxvij lib. xiijs. iiijd. Item, be Robert Stenart, in mill of Aird, Lxxxxvij lib. iiijs. vid. Item, be Audro Griman, in Capath, xv lib. Item, be Red Wm. Haggart thair, xxvij lib. Item, be William Haggart, elder, thair, xxix lib. Item, be Jhon Baxter, in Brydiestone, xliij lib. xijs. Item, be Elspeth Brydie, in Gowrdie mylne, je xli lib. vjs. viijd. Item, be Isobell Buroch, in Insche Stuthill, xvi lib. Item, be Thomas Kilgour thair, xxx lib. Item, be Jhon Cadell thair, xxiiij lib. iiijs. Item, be James Heriott thair, 25 lib. Item, be William Haggart thair, Lxxxv lib. Item, be Alexr. Stirtoune thair, xviij lib. xvs. Item, be James Stirtoun thair, xxvij lib. xs. Item, be Colline Campbell thair, xlviij lib. Item, be James Wilkie thair, xxxix lib. 1s. viiid. Item, be James Mories thair, x lib. Item, be William Darling thair, xx lib. Item, be George Pecok thair, xij lib. xs. Item, be Jhon McWilliam thair, x lib. Item, be Thomas Pecok thair, iiij lib. 15s. Item, be William Kae, Lxxi lib. ijs. Item, be James Laycok thair, Lxxij lib. Item, be Jhon Kae thair, Lxxij lib. Mair restand be the tenantis of the baronie of Insche Stuthill, of thair half-yearis dewtie cropt 1651, over and above the allowance given to them of thair quarteris, iije Liij lib. Item, be the heritouris of the shyre of Mernis, jm vic Lxvi lib. 18s. 4d. Item, for the annuel rent thairof since Marche, jm vjc, and threttie nyne yearis, jm iic lib. Item, be Jhon Barcklay sometyme of Syd, im ije lib.

"Summa of the saidis debtes, vim je lii lib. xvis. xd.

"Summa Inventar and debtes, viijm ije Lx lib. 10s. 4d.

"DEBTES AWAND BE THE DEAD.

"Imprimis, to Thomas Lyall, cook, xiij lib. vis. viijd. Item, to David Thomson, a servant, xiij lib. vis. viijd. Item, to William Heres, servant, for twa yearis fie, xxvi lib. 13s. iiijd. Item, to John Duncan, servant, twa yearis fie, xxvj lib. 13s. 4d. Item, to James Smith, twa yearis fie, xxvj lib. 13s. 4d. Item, to George Black, xx lib. Item, to Jhon Hird, twa yearis fie, 26 lib. 13s. 4d. Item, to the four servant women, xl lib. Item, to Jhon Zeaman, apothacarie in Dundie, xl lib. Item, to Jean Winton thair, ij lib. Item, to Magdelen Gray thair, xxvj lib.

"Summa of the saidis debtes, ijc Lxx lib. vis. 8d.

"Summa frie gear debtes, deducit, viiim ije xvi lib. ijs. ijd.

"To be devydit in three partis, ilk part is ijm vije Liij lib. xvjs. 9d.

"CONFIRMATION.

"Collonell William Daniell, etc., and Mr Jhone Nairne, deputt, etc., Ratifies approves this present Testament dative and Inventar etc.; and als confirmes the said James Strachan, executor dative to his said vmquhile father. With power, etc. Who hes

maid faith, and found James Strachane in kirktoune of Letheudie, cautioner, etc., for whose
relieff, the said executor has become actit, etc. And protestit to be hard to eik, etc. Sub-
scriuit att Perth, the eleventh day of August, 1653 years."

Pursuant to a provision in the contract by which his father had purchased Inchtuthill (see *supra*), James Strachan of Inchtuthill granted, on the 16th May 1654, to "Mary Ramsay, his mother," a bond for "2000 merks yearly furth of the lands and barony of Inchtuthill, and that in consideration of the said Mary Ramsay having been infeft and seised for that amount, by James Strachan of Fettercairn his father" (Register of Deeds, vol. 615). Mary Ramsay, wife of James Strachan, first of Inchtuthill, was a daughter of David Ramsay of Balmain, father of Sir Gilbert Ramsay, Bart. She married, secondly, Alexander Buchan of Auchmacoy, in the county of Aberdeen.

James Strachan, eldest son of James Strachan of Inchtuthill, succeeded to his father's estates in 1651. He was living at Inchtuthill in 1654, when he addressed to his future brother-in-law, Sir John Forbes of Waterton, the following letter:

"The Leard of Watertoune.

"RIGHT HONOURABLE,—Its now of so a long a tyme since a lyne has been interchanged betwixt us, that I think we wax outt of acquaintance. I have been this long whyll at, and am bott lately returned from Edinburgh. I shal, through God's help, see you att your owne honse in March, for I am to bee the length of the Mearnes for to cause cast our peats and doe uther things incumbant to our removall. I hope yee will nott bee any way from home through all that monith of March, butt I may find you when I come. I hope, and am confident, ye'll also mynd the contents of my former letters, and against my coming have something done with my servaent Petrie; and if Bailzie Skeen receave a meal [chest] of myne full of wrytts from David Strachan [1] (as is like he'll doe), I pray you cause keep them carefully for me, for, till Whitsonday, I intend not to bring them away, because I'll heir a folly [hire a young horse] first to bring them heer, and then so shortly re-carry them to Thorntoune. I pray remember my most entyre love and services to my good mother, to your lady and her sister, and to your owne sisters, and to Auchmacoy and his lady.[2] I was

---

[1] Probably his younger brother.
[2] The first wife of Alexander Buchan of Auchmacoy is here referred to.

so haisted that I could nott wrytt to none of them, and onely add the subscryber to be—
Your most affectionatt brother to serve you,   J. STRAH[ANE].
  "Inchstuthill, the 1st of February 165⅞."[1]

The allusion to Thornton in the preceding letter shows that the writer then possessed a portion of the lands. In 1658, as " Mr James Strachan, laird of Thorntoune," he is described as contributing to the fund for rebuilding King's College, Aberdeen (Records of King's College). As nearest heir-male to Sir Alexander Strachan, the second baronet, he succeeded to the baronetcy of Thornton in 1659, and at once proceeded to negotiate a complete restoration of the ancestral estate. In 1661 he sold to his relative, James, Earl of Middleton, the barony of Inchtuthill. The instrument of sale is a contract between the earl and himself, bearing date 20th April 1661, and which was registered in the Books of Council and Session, 9th July 1705. In the introduction are these words: "John, Earle of Middleton, Lord Cleirmonth and Fettercairn, on the one part, and Sir James Strachan of Thornton, knight baronet, with advyse, express consent, and assent of Marie Ramsay, his mother, and of Alexander Buchan of Auchmacoy, now her husband." The narrative proceeds: "Forsan meickle as by contract and appointment made betwixt the said noble Earle, John, Earle of Middleton, on the one pairt, and the said Sir James Strachan on the other pairt, of the date of thir presents, the said noble Earle has sold, etc., to the said Sir James, his airs, etc., his towns and lands of Over and Nether Balmakewan, with houses, etc., upon the water of Esk, *alias* called the Northwater; and also all and haill the milne of Over Balmakewan, *alias* called the milne of Luther, with mutters, etc., lying in the thanedom and parochine of Aberluthnot and

---

[1] Memoranda relating to the Family of Forbes of Waterton, from a MS. of the deceased John Forbes (b. 1754, who was served heir to the last Thomas Forbes of Waterton in 1775), printed solely for the use of members of the family. Aberdeen, 1857, 4to, p. 61.

Sheriffdom of Kincardine and sicklike; all and sundry the townes and lands of Over and Nether Erigstounes and pendicle thereof, called the auld Walkmilne of Thorntoun, the towns and lands of New Thorntoun, Milntoun of Thorntoun," etc. One of the two witnesses to this instrument is "Sir John Strachan, knight."

Respecting Sir John Strachan, the following resolution was on the 27th December 1643 passed by the Magistrates and Town Council of Aberdeen: "The quhilk day the provost, baillies, and counsell, all in ane voice, but contradiction, electit, nominat, and chusit Captain John Straquhan, to be captan and leader of the company of soiours levied, and to be levied, out of this burghe, for the present expedition vnto England, and ordanes him immediatlie efter the dait heirof to enter with his charge in training and dreilling of the said company, and vsing of all militarie discipline over thame, conform to the order vseit in sic caices" (Records of Burgh of Aberdeen, Edinb. 1872, 4to, p. 11). On the 7th January 1661, Sir John Strachan received the office of Chamberlain of the Earldom of Ross and Lordship of Ardmannoch, with all benefits arising therefrom, for his services to the king and his father, which office was before, in the year 1665, granted him along with the office of Receiver of His Majesty's Rents. He received a gift of the office of Third Receiver of the Rents and Casualties of the Scottish Exchequer, on the 31st December 1660 (Reg. Sec. Sig., vol. i., fols. 108, 109). Sir John Strachan received on the 25th August 1662, a gift of "the goods and gear formerly belonging to umquhil Ninian Dunbar of Grangehill," put to the horn (Reg. Sec. Sig., vol. i., fol. 127). On the 22d December 1662, he had a charter of the lands of Newton of Wrangham, parish of Culsamond, Aberdeenshire, and others which formerly belonged to George Gordon of Newton, held by him in fee-farm of the late Sir William Forbes of Craigievar, Knight (Reg. Mag. Sig., lib. lx., No. 182). He had, on the 24th August 1663, gift of the goods and entire property of James Gordon, sometime of Newton, now in the king's hands by reason of the said James Gordon's non-appearance for trial for the murder of Alexander Lyndsay of Williamstown (Reg. Sec. Sig., vol. i., fol. 224*b*).

On the 24th January 1654, James Strachan, second of Inchtuthill, subsequently Sir James Strachan of Thornton, Baronet, married his cousin Elizabeth, third daughter of Thomas Forbes of Waterton, by his wife Jean, daughter of David Ramsay of Balmain, and sister of Sir Gilbert Ramsay, Bart. (Parish Register of Ellon). In the Waterton Papers, the marriage-contract is noticed thus: "1654, *5th January.*—Contract of marriage between James Strachan of Inchestuthell and Elizabeth Forbes, with consent of her mother, Jean Ramsay, by which he settles the life-rent of his lands on her, after the death of his mother, Margaret [Mary] Ramsay, in consideration of a portion of 8000 merks." Elizabeth Forbes, Lady Strachan, died on the 10th January 1661, soon after giving birth to her third child; she was in her twenty-fifth year. To her memory, Sir James Strachan, her husband, erected an elegant marble tomb in the family burial aisle at Marykirk. It is inscribed thus:

"Epicedium thrœnodicum in memoriam fœminæ lectissimæ, Dominæ Elizabethæ Forbesæ, Dominæ a Thornton, æternitatis candidatæ præmio meritorum dignissima, puerpera, immaturo fato correpta est, dum annum ætatis vigesimum quintum agebat, die decimo Ianuarij 1661: Cujus fragrantissimæ memoriæ, licet abunde monumentis omni ære perennioribus abunde satis litatum sit, hoc tamen magnifico mausoleo, parentandum curavit conjunx ipsius pullatus. D. Iacobus Strahanus a Thorntonæ, eques auratus.

Siste, viator, habes summi monumenta doloris;
Virtutis tumulum, pieridumque vides
Omnibus una fuit brevis hæc, quam conspicis ætas;
Lux nuper patriæ nunc levis umbra jacet.
Aurea si tantas fudere crepuscula laudes,
Luxisset quanto sidere quale jubar!
Quanta fuit pietas! quam stemmatis æmula virtus!

> Euthea mens, roseus quam sine sente sinus!
> Quantus et oris honos! Phœnix vixitque caditque,
> Qualem non poterant reddere lustra dewm;
> At matura polo cedidit Christoque; quid ultra?
> Ignavi numerant sæcula, facta boni.
> Mors ipsa non separabit."

By his wife, Elizabeth Forbes, Sir James Strachan was father of a son, James, and two daughters. In the Waterton Papers is the following entry: "1665.—Jeane Ramsay summons Sir James Strachan of Thornetoun, complaining that soon after the death of Elizabeth Forbes, his wife, he had neglected his affairs and abandoned his three children—James, Jean, and ——[1] Strachan—whom the said Jean Ramsay, their grandmother, had taken in and educated. She requires that he should make her an allowance for the same." By the neglect of his affairs subsequent to his wife's death, Sir James Strachan involved his estate, and impoverished his fortune. On the 30th November 1661, he granted a bond for 2000 merks of borrowed money to Margaret Wood, relict of John Strachan of Hauchhead (Reg. of Deeds, vol. xii.). On the 29th November 1662, he gave a bond to Robert Ronald, burgess in Montrose, for the loan of £310, 15s. (Reg. of Deeds, vol. viii.). On the 19th February 1663, he granted an obligation for £448 to George Suthie, merchant-burgess of Edinburgh (Reg. of Deeds, vol. viii., Dalrymple Office). On the 26th November he gave a bond for 239 merks to John Gray, merchant-burgess of Montrose (Reg. of Deeds, vol. xii.). On the 25th May 1664, he acknowledged the loan of £138 by a bond to Robert Taylor, provost of Montrose (Reg. of Deeds, vol. xvi.). On the 16th March 1665, he granted a bond for £223 to Sir James Ramsay of Benholme (Reg. of Deeds, vol. xxi.). He gave a bond for 200 merks, on the 21st May 1670,

---

[1] The name of the younger daughter was Grizel. She married the Rev. Ludovick Grant, minister of Duthill, and had a son Ludovick (Reg. Mag. Sig., lib. xvi., No. 103, fol. 170).

to Mr David Thares, and on the 8th March 1672, a bond to Alexander Mackintosh, notary in Montrose, for £180 (Reg. of Deeds, vols. xxviii. and xxxiv.).

Sir James Strachan was in 1661 appointed a commissioner to assist in raising the annuity of £40,000 for Charles II. (Acta Parl. Scot., vii. 94). He enlarged Thornton Castle, which was originally constructed in 1531. In the Register of the Privy Seal (vol. ii., p. 285) is contained a ratification of a charter by the Earl of Middleton to Sir James Strachan, of the lands of Nether Balmakewan, etc., in the parish of Marykirk, and confirming a charter by Thomas Allardice, tutor of Allardice, "to Sir James, of the lands of Hauchheid (except such parts thereof as were disponed by the late Sir Alexander Strachan, formerly of Thornetoun, and the late John Strachan, formerly of Hauchheid, to Sir Francis Ogilvy of New Grange), of date 15th July 1659; and of another charter by James Keith, formerly of Caldhame, to the said Sir James Strachan, of the lands of Caldhame, of date 10th June 1662, and confirming to James Strachan, only lawful son of the said Sir James, begotten betwixt him and the late Elizabeth Forbes, his first spouse, the barony of Thornton."

James Strachan, described in the charter of June 1662 as "only lawful son of Sir James Strachan of Thornton, and his wife Elizabeth Forbes," entered the University of King's College, Aberdeen, in 1670; he is designated in the Matriculation Register of the University as "James Straquhan, junior, de Thornton." On the 9th June 1669, a contract was entered into between Sir James Strachan of Thornton, as "tutor and administrator-at-law for James Strachan, his eldest lawful son, on the one part, and Robert Forbes of Newtoun, and Barbara Forbes, his third daughter, on the other part, for the marriage of the said James and Barbara." Her dowry is named as 8000 merks. The parties to be married are infeft in the lands and barony of Thornton, reserving liferent of a portion thereof to Sir James Strachan, and his mother, Mary Ramsay, Lady Auchmacoy (Deeds in Durie Office, General Register House, vol. xxiv.). When this contract was executed, James Strachan—described as "eldest," but in reality the only son of Sir James Strachan, third baronet of Thornton—was about fourteen years old; but as the contract is registered on the 16th November 1670, it is probable that the marriage was delayed till that year. Doubtless the union was arranged between the families with the view of preserving the Thornton estates, which seem to have been wasted through the improvidence of the third baronet. Having further involved himself, Sir James, with consent of Robert Forbes of Newtoun, who had advanced large sums on the estates, resigned them for re-conveyance. Accordingly the lands were, by a charter under the Great Seal, dated at Whitehall, 31st October 1681, conveyed to James Strachan, only son of Sir James, "fiar of Thornton," and "Barbara Forbes, his spouse, and the longest liver of them in liferent." Of this charter an abstract follows :—

"Charter granted by King Charles the Second to James Strachan, fiar of Thornetoune, and Barbara Forbes, his spouse, and the longest liver of them two (to the said Barbara in liferent only, and in satisfaction of all she could claim, in virtue of her contract of marriage or otherwise), and to the heirs and assignees whomsoever of the said James, in fee heritably and irredeemably, under the reservation under specified, of all and whole the lands of Miltoune of Thornetoune, New Thorntoune, and Brandisleyes, with the pertinents, lying within the Sheriffdom of Kincardine: And in like manner to the said James Strachan, fiar of Thornetoune, his heirs and assignees whomsoever, all and whole the Mains of Thornetoune, with the tower, fortalice, manor-place, etc.; and the pertinents, the lands called Neather Longhaugh, Bark-planting, Carter-yairds, Aikers of Bent, and the moss thereof, Haughhead, Burgertoun, Haughills of Thornetoune, Midmaines, with mills, multures, and sequels thereof, Over and Neather Brigtounes and Whitefaulds, with houses, biggings, etc., lying within the said Sheriffdom of Kincardine—all united and annexed into a free barony to be called the Barony of Thornetoun: Reserving always to Mary Ramsay, lady of Auchincoy, her right of liferent thereof to be provided to her according to the rights and securities granted her thereupon. Which whole lands, barony, mill, and others above-written, with the pertinents, belonged before to Sir James Strachane, elder of Thornetoun, and Robert

Forbes of Newtoun, or the survivor of them, in liferent during the life of the said Sir James Strachan; and to the said Sir James Strachan heritably in fee, holden immediately of the Crown, and were by them and their procurators specially constituted to that effect duly and lawfully resigned in the hands of the lords and others, commissioners of his Highness' treasury and exchequer, having power to receive resignations, and to grant new infeftments thereupon, as in the hands of his Majesty, immediate lawful superior thereof, in favour and for new infeftment of the said lands of Miltoune of Thornetoune, New Thornetoune, and Braudislayes, with the pertinents, to be given by the king under his great seal to the said James Strachan and Barbara Forbes, spouses, and the longer liver of them, in conjunct fee and liferent (for the said Barbara Forbes's liferent only, etc., as above), and the said James Strachan's heirs whomsoever and assignees in fee; and for new infeftment of all the remanent foresaid lands and others above written, with the pertinents, to be granted under the great seal to the before-mentioned James Strachan, fiar of Thornetoune, his heirs and assignees, heritably and irredeemably, in such due and competent form, always under the reservation above specified, as authentic instruments subscribed thereon, in the hands of John Campbell, writer to our Signet, notary public, of date the 15th day of July 1681, more fully purport. And further, his Majesty, for the good and faithful service done to him and his progenitors by the said Sir James, and James Strachan, and their predecessors, and for other causes, of new gives and grants to the said Sir James Strachan and Barbara Forbes, spouses, etc. [as above], and to the foresaid James Strachan [as above] . . . the said lands all united and annexed as said is, with all rights, etc., Renouncing and overgiving, etc., from him and his successors to and in favour of the said James Strachan and his foresaids, etc. And further, of new unites and annexes the foresaid lands into a whole and free barony, now, and in all time coming, to be called The Barony of Thorntoun: Ordaining the castle, tower, fortalice, and manor-place of Thornetoune to be the principal messuage of the said barony, and that a single seisin taken there or upon the ground of any other part of the foresaid lands by the said James, etc., shall be sufficient, etc., To have and to hold, etc., in fee, heritage, and free barony for ever, etc.: Paying therefor yearly, the said James Strachan and his foresaids to the king and his successors, the taxt ward duties underwritten, used, and wont to be paid before the resignation above written—viz., for the foresaids lands and Barony of Thornetoun (except the said lands of Bent and Moss thereof) the sum of fifty pounds Scots yearly during the whole time of ward and non-entry of either of them; with the like sum of 50 lib. for the relief thereof when it shall happen, and paying for the marriage of the heirs and successors of the said James Strachan the sum of one thousand merks, with one suit at the head court annually, to be held within the said Sheriffdom of Kincardine after the expiration of the foresaid ward and non-entry only. And for the said Aikers of Bent and Moss thereof, the sum of 13s. 4d. Scots yearly during the whole space of ward and non-entry foresaid, with 13s. 4d. of relief when it shall happen; with ten merks for the marriage of the heirs and successors of the said James Strachane: To which duties, as the value of the taxt of the said ward, non-entry, relief, and marriage respecting the foresaid lands and Barony of Thornetoun, with the pertinents, were taxt and restricted by a charter granted by our royal grandfather in favour of umquhile Sir Alexander Strachan of Thornetoune (thereon designed

Alexander Strachan of Thorntoune), of date the 25th day of August 1616. And further, willing and granting that it shall be lawful to the heirs-apparent and successors of the said James Strachan, from time to time in all time coming, whatever be their age, to be served and retoured infeft and seized in the said lands and Barony of Thornetoun in taxt ward, notwithstanding that the said heirs and successors be minors, etc. And finally, promising on the word of a prince to cause this charter to be ratified in this present or in the next ensuing Parliament. (Follows a precept of seisin.) In witness whereof, etc." (Reg. Mag. Sig., lib. lxviii., No. 65).

The arrangement provided by this charter did not long subsist, for by a decreet of the Lords of Council and Session on the 28th March 1683, the lands of Thornton were, for £13,924, 14s. 8d., adjudged from Sir James Strachan, Bart., James Strachan, his eldest son, and Barbara Forbes, his spouse, in favour of Robert Forbes, styled " of Ludquharn." By Robert Forbes, the lands were, on the 5th August 1685, disponed to his son William, "reserving to Mary Ramsay the usufruct of the said lands for her lifetime, and also reserving to James Strachan, junior, and Barbara Forbes, his spouse, the heritable right of the lands of New Thornton and other portions of the said estate." With consent of Sir James Strachan, James, his son, and Barbara Forbes, spouse of the latter, the lands of Thornton were, in 1685-6, conveyed to James Forbes of Saach, to whom, on the 2d April 1694, they were confirmed by charter (Reg. Mag. Sig., lib. lxx., 65; lib. lxxiii., 78; Waterton Family Papers).

Sir James Strachan, Bart., died in 1686. He was predeceased by his son, who had a son, James, who died in infancy. Barbara Forbes, wife of James Strachan, younger of Thornton, also died young. A memorial tablet in the Thornton burial aisle in the church of Marykirk, bearing date 1690, commemorates " Philip Forbes de Thornton;" and in the list of Commissioners of Supply for the county of Kincardine in the same year, is mentioned " James Forbes of Thornetoun " (Acta Parl. Scot., vol. ix., p. 142). The latter, in the Pedigree Chart of Forbes of Waterton, is described as second brother of Elizabeth Forbes, wife of Sir James

Strachan, Bart., and as "of Saach, afterwards of Thornton" (Waterton Family Papers). On the 5th January 1700, a charter was granted to Mr Robert Forbes, advocate, of the lands of New Thornton, etc., as adjudged from William Forbes of Ludquharn in 1692 for a debt of £1503 (Reg. Mag. Sig., lib. lxxvi., No. 17). On the 12th February 1715, Thomas Forbes of Thornton received a charter of adjudication under the Great Seal :

"Of all and whole the lands and barony of Thornton, all and whole the lands of Caldhame and Saughburne, with all their pertinents lying, within the parish of Aberluthnot [Marykirk] and sheriffdom of Kincardine, which said lands formerly belonged in heritage to James Strachan, eldest son and heir of the deceased James Strachan of Thorntoun, and grandson and heir to Sir James Strachan of Thornton, his grandfather, and which, through a decreit of adjudication, obtained on the 1st December 1708, at the instance of Mary Strachan, lawful daughter of the deceased Sir James Strachan of Thorntoun, against the said James Strachan as heir to his said father and grandfather, were apprised and decreed to belong to the said Mary Strachan and her heirs and assignees in heritage, for default of payment of the sum of £7212, 13s. 4d. Scots, of principal, annual rents, and liquidat expenses (the price of the redemption deducted); which said lands and decreit of adjudication, with the infeftments, warrants, and the accumulated sum above mentioned, were assigned by the said Mary Strachan to, and in favour of, the said Thomas Forbes of Thorntoun, by her disposition and assignation, dated 10th May 1711 : Which said lands and others above mentioned, by another decreit of adjudication of the date the 21st June 1710, at the instance of Master Ludovic Grant, son of the deceased Master Ludovic Grant, minister of the Gospel at Duthell, lawfully procreated between him and Grizel Strachan, his wife, daughter of unquhile Sir James Strachan of Thorntoun, as having right by the assignation of his said mother, against the said James Strachan, eldest lawful son and heir of unquhile James Strachan, his father, and grandson and heir of the said Sir James Strachan, his grandfather, were adjudicated and declared to pertain to the said Master Ludovick Grant, his heirs and assignees, for default of payment of the sum (redemption deducted) of £3910 Scots, owed and not payed, as contained in the said decreit of adjudication; which lands, infeftments, warrants, sums, etc., were assigned by the said Master Ludovic Grant to, and in favour of, the said Thomas Forbes, his heirs and assignees in heritage, as his heir and assignee, by his disposition and assignation of the dates the 9th March and 27th May 1713" (Reg. Mag. Sig., lib. xvi., No. 103, fol. 170).

The estate of Thornton remained in possession of the House of Forbes till 1720, when it was acquired by the family of Fullerton, a member of which sold it in 1786 to Lord Gardenstone, an eminent lawyer and patron of literature. By Francis Garden of Troup, son and successor of Lord Gardenstone, the property was sold to Alexander Crombie of Phesdo; it is now possessed by his son, Alexander Crombie, Esq., of Lincoln's Inn, Barrister-at-law.

On the death of Sir James Strachan, third baronet of Thornton, the succession to the baronetcy devolved on Mr James Strachan, minister of Keith.[1]

He studied at King's College, Aberdeen, and there graduated Master of Arts on the 28th March 1660. In the College Register he is styled "M. Jacobus Strachanus, a Thorntoune comarchus, Merniensis." Obtaining licence as a probationer, he was presented by Sir John Forbes, Bart. of Craigievar, to the parish of Keith, and was ordained to the charge on the 25th July 1665.

In the Records of the Synod of Moray in 1686, he is styled "Mr James Strachan," and in the Baptismal Register of Keith, he is, on the 6th January 1687, described as "Sir James Strachan of Thornton, minister;" in the interval he had succeeded to the baronetcy. The family estates, as we have seen, were alienated, but the new baronet possessed the lands of Pittendreich, formerly a part of the Thornton estate. His plurality of dignities was celebrated in these lines:

> " The beltit knicht o' Thornton,
> An' laird o' Pittendreich;
> An' Maister James Strachan,
> Minister o' Keith."

Of his cure, Sir James Strachan was deprived by the Privy Council, 7th November 1689, for not reading the proclamation of the Estates, refusing to pray for King William and Queen Mary, and praying for the restoration of the late king (Privy Council Records). Encouraged by the adherents of the exiled House, he established a meeting-house at

[1] Probably a nephew of the third baronet — the son of a younger brother.

Keith, and was subjected to popular violence. His library was scattered, many of his books being tossed into the street. A few odd volumes are preserved in the vestry of the parish church. He died at Inverness in 1715 (Fasti Eccl. Scot., vol. iii., p. 206).

Sir James Strachan married Katherine Ross, who died on the 6th April 1689. A monument to her memory within the old church of Keith, is thus inscribed: "Sub scamno D^{d.} Kinminnitie cineres lectissimæ feminæ D. Kath. Rossæ D. de Thorntone, cuius etiamsi fragrantissimæ memoriæ monumentis omni ære perenniorib., abunde satis litatum sit hoc tamen mausoeleo parentandum duxit coniunx ipsius pullatus D. Jac. Strachanus de Thornt., huius ecclesiæ pastor. Obiit puerpera 6th Apr. anno 1689 conquiescunt et hic Gul., Rob., et Joshue Strachanus filii eorum." Of the reverend baronet's six sons, three, William, Robert, and Joshua, died in childhood. James, his eldest surviving son, fell in the Rebellion of 1715, fighting under the Earl of Mar, in the cause of the exiled Royal House. William, second of the name, succeeded to the baronetcy on the death of his father.[1] Francis, the third son, followed the fortunes of the exiled Royal House; he took orders in the Church of Rome, and became rector of the National College at Douay in 1734. He latterly succeeded to the baronetcy (Fasti Eccl. Scot., vol. iii., p. 201; the Rev. Dr Oliver's Society of Jesus, p. 38).

The Rev. Dr Oliver, in his work on "The Society of Jesus,"[2] mentions a father and two sons as successive baronets of Thornton. "Alexander Strachan," he writes, "was the eldest son of Sir Alexander

---

[1] The existence of this baronet is proved by the following entry in the Baptismal Register of Marykirk: "*July 21st*, 1715.—Baptized William, natural son to Sir William Strachan of Thorntoune and Margaret Spark."

[2] Collections towards illustrating the Biography of the Scotch, English, and Irish Members of the Society of Jesus. By the Rev. Dr Oliver, St Nicholas Priory, Exeter. Lond. 1844, 8vo, p. 38.

Strachan (the sixth baronet of Nova Scotia), by his wife Jane Bremner of Attenbury; and on the death of his father succeeded to the title, with its slender income. This worthy Jesuit had travelled much, and was universally esteemed and respected for his solid and unaffected virtues and most amiable manners. He retired in his old age to the English College at Liege, where he died 3d January 1793. The title descended to his only brother Robert, a most devout layman, and a gentleman of unblemished honour and integrity. He died at Exeter, 3d April 1826, æt. 89, and was buried at St Nicholas Chapel in that city."

Sir Alexander Strachan, described by Dr Oliver as "sixth baronet of Nova Scotia," was probably grandson of the Rev. Sir James Strachan, fourth baronet of Thornton. In the "Book of Caerlaverock," Mr William Fraser presents the following letter, as addressed by "Father Sir Alexander Strachan" to William Maxwell Constable of Everinghame:

"KIRKCONNELL, 17th February 1781.

"HONOUR'D SIR,—I was honoured with the favor of yours, with an enclosed from Mr Blundell. I am much obliged to you for the good testimony you are pleased to give of me, tho' our friend Mr Berrington is pleased to say in his pamphlet that the priests who travell with young gentlemen are both ignorant and self-sufficient. I have written to Mr Blundell. Whether he will accept of my proposal or not, I cannot tell; for my own part, I rather wish he would not; as I am now past the meridian of life, travelling is not what I relish much at present. However, as I always looked upon the education of young gentlemen as the most important duty of one of my calling, especially in this country, where Catholic families are the pillars that support the tottering remains of religion, I have offered to take the charge of his son, provided he chuses to settle upon me the small sum of fourty pounds sterling a year for the short remainder of my life.[1] As our colleges and houses abroad where the aged and infirm might find a comfortable refuge are taken from us, it would be very imprudent in me, now past fifty, to relinquish a certain and comfortable maintenance, tho' without a fixed salary, and to expose myself to the dangers of want and necessity when old age comes on, with all its disagreeable retinue. Lord Selkirk, I hear, Mr Herron, and others, are called by summons to appear before the committee for the

---

[1] Sir Alexander Strachan was sometime tutor in the family of John Webb Weston, Esq.

Kirkcudbright election. His Lordship is very ill-pleased, as he has always been scrupulously nice about interfering in elections; but Mr Gordon, who no doubt is in town, will give you better account of all this. Be pleased to tell him, with my best compliments, that he has the warmest wishes of the very great majority of all ranks in this country. The great drover, Mr Tait, being declared a bankrupt, has thrown both the gentlemen and farmers into great distress; even the cautious Munshes is taken in for some small matter. Everybody seems to express great pleasure that Campbeltown is fined in £300 sterling for refusing to inroll some of Mr Gordon's voters, he being under-sheriff. We have had a fine open winter here; the grass is as green as I have seen it in April some other years. Sir James and Lady Riddell still at the Mains. The two young gentlemen speak of waiting upon you at Grosvenor Place in a few days, on their way to their respective regiments. Our Dumfries newsmonger, who is a great American, makes a pompous description in his paper of the rejoicings made at the Bridge-end for Lord G. Gordon; but the fact is that only one farmer, a violent American, and a few bare-legged boys gathered together by him, assembled and made a paltry bonfire on the Corbley Hill [which] belongs to you; no person above the rank of a beggar or a cobbler's apprentice joined the band. You will have seen in the papers the death of Lord Hopeton, who was cut off by a dropsy in the breast. Nothing new in this part of the country. I beg you will please to present my best and most respectable compliments to Lady Winifred and —— Constable, and all enquiring friends; and I have the honour of being, with the most sincere regard, honour'd sir, your most obedient humble servant,

"ALEX. STRACHAN."

"Mrs Maxwell and sons join in compliments to you and Lady Winifred. Mr William is still in a poor way of health, on account of his making new teeth."

Robert Strachan, the younger brother, was clerk in Gandolfe's Bank, Exeter; and latterly lived in retirement. He died unmarried in 1826.

To show the descent of the next baronet of Thornton, it is necessary to recapitulate. In the will of James Strachan of Monboddo, who died on the 10th July 1614, are named his two surviving sons, Robert and David. The eldest son of James Strachan had, we have seen, predeceased him, leaving a son, James, who, as an Edinburgh trader, acquired the lands of Fettercairn and barony of Inchtuthill, and who became father of Sir James Strachan, the third baronet. This baronet being predeceased by his son and grandson, the male representation of the House and of the baronetcy of Thornton devolved on the eldest male issue of Robert, second son of James Strachan of Monboddo, the third baronet's great-grandfather.

Robert Strachan studied medicine, and at first sought practice as a physician at Stonehaven. Having excited hostile feeling on the part of William Hay of Ury, a landowner in the neighbourhood, he was revengefully pursued by that individual. Consequent on a violent attempt upon his life made by Hay on the 22d October 1612, Dr Robert Strachan made a complaint to the Privy Council. The early proceedings in the case are in the Privy Council Records detailed in these terms:

"*Apud Edinburgh tertio die mensis Decembris* 1612.

"Anent oure soverane lordis lettres reasit at the instance of maister Robert Stranchane doctor of medecine makand mentioun, That quhair vpoun the xxvj day of October last William Hay of Vrie and Thomas Anchinleck sometyme servitour to the Erll of Orknay boith bodin in feir of weir with swordis daggeris gantillatis and vtheris wapponis invasiue, come to the dwelling house of Andro Kellie in Stanehyve suirlie beleveing that the said complenare had bene within the said house, and thair the said Laird of Vrie and Thomas Anchinleck for thair forder suirtie that the said complenair not eschaip vupersewit of his lyff the said Laird of Vrie stayit watcheing in the cloise and the said Thomas Anchinleck euterit in the said house with a drawin swerd in his hand dang and brak vp the chalmer duris of the said house stoggit beddis and vsit all meanis possible to haif apprehendit the said complenair of purpois and intentioun to haue slane him, and finding thame selffis disapointit of thair inteudit purpois and haueing gottin intelligence that the said complenair had repairit to the lynkis of the said toun of Stanehyve to recreat him selff, The saidis personis come directlie to the saidis lynkis quhair the said complenair wes in sober maner as saidis of purpois and intentioun to haue slane him quhilk they had not faillit to haue done wer not the said complenair be the counsaill of some gentilmen who wer present with him withdrew him selff of the saidis lynkis committing thairthrow ane maist appin and avowit appressioun vpoun the said complenair To the heich and proud contempt of his maiesteis auctoritie and lawis ffor the quhilk the saidis personis aucht to be persewit and pvnist in thair personis and goodis To the terrour of vtheris to commit the lyke heirefter And anent the chairge gevin to the said William Hay of Vrie To haue compeirit personalie before the Lordis of secrite counsale this present Third day of December instant To haue answerit to this complaint and to haue hard and sene sic ordour tane thairanent as appertenit vndir the pane of rebellioun and puting of him to the horne, With certificatioun to him and he failzeit lettres sould be direct simpliciter to put him thairto, Lyke as at mair lenth is contenit in the saidis lettres executionis and indorsationis thairof, Quhilkis being callit and the said persewair compeirand personalie and the said William Hay of Vrie being oftymes callit and not compeirand, The Lordis of secrite counsale thairfore ordainis lettres to be direct chairgeing officiaris of airmes To pas and denunce the said William Hay of Vrie his maiesteis rebell and put him to his heynes horne and to eschete, etc." (Regist. Sec. Concilii, Decreta).

Criminal proceedings against the laird of Ury were withdrawn; but the assailed physician seems to have removed from a locality where his personal safety was endangered. It is sufficiently remarkable to find that in less than a year after this violent attack had been made upon himself, he, on the 19th August 1613, joined his relative, Alexander Strachan of Thornton, in forcibly wresting a legal document from Captain Alexander Wishart of Phesdo—an act which also came before the Privy Council (see *supra*).

From Stonehaven, Dr Robert Strachan removed to Montrose in 1613 or the following year. Described as "lawfull sone of umq^ll James Strathauchan of Monbodo," he obtained sasine "of a rig of arable land" at Montrose, 26th September 1617 (Montrose Register of Sasines, 1613-1630, fol. 59). On the 21st May 1618, he obtained a charter of the town and lands of Edneston from David Tulloch of Craignestoun, Alexander Tulloch, fiar thereof, and Jean Strachan, spouse of the said David—the witnesses being John and George Strachan, sons of the late Alexander Strachan of Thorntoun, and Alexander Strachan, servitor to Sir Alexander Strachan of Thorntoun, Knight. On this charter he took infeftment on the 10th June 1618, and is in the instrument of sasine described as "an honorable man, Robert Strachane, indweller in Montrose, son of the late James Strachan of Monboddow" (General Register of Sasines, vol. i., fol. 368).

In 1624, Dr Robert Strachan was charged before the Privy Council as having aided his relative, Sir Alexander Strachan of Thornton, in removing certain jewels from the house of the Earl Marischal, such being claimed as her property by the widow of the fifth earl, who had espoused Sir Alexander Strachan as her second husband (see *supra*). In January 1627, Dr Robert Strachan acted as procurator for his niece, Christian Arbuthnot, relict of Mr Andrew Strathauchan, parson at Dun (Montrose Register of Sasines, vol. 1613-1630, fol. 126). A disposition by Sir Alexander Strachan of Thornton, dated 19th July 1628, in favour of James Strachan of Fettercairn, bears to have been executed "with consent of Mr Robert Strachan, doctor of physic," and John Strachan, uncle of the granter (General Reg. of Deeds, vol. ccccxix.). In a charter dated at Edinburgh, 13th March 1637, whereby the lands of the Little Park of Kincardine and others were granted to James Strachan of Kincardine, Dr Robert Strachan is named as having consented to their being alienated by Sir Alexander Strachan (Reg. Mag. Sig., lib. lv., 315). In the Burgh Records of Montrose, he is mentioned as alive in 1656, and as "umq^{ll} Doctor Robert Strachane" in August 1659. Dr Robert Strachan married Agnes Troup, whom he liferented in a house in Montrose, which he purchased from Sir Alexander Falconer of Halkerston, 26th November 1624 (Montrose Reg. of Sasines, vol. 1613-1630, fol. 102). He was father of two sons and three daughters—Christian, the second daughter, baptized 22d March 1624, and Catherine, third daughter, baptized 28th April 1628, died in infancy (Montrose Baptismal Register). Jean, the eldest daughter, married, 19th May 1643, Andrew Jameson, merchant in Montrose; she and her husband were, on the 8th December 1643, infeft by Dr Robert Strachan in his dwelling-house, reserving his liferent; they succeeded thereto on his death (Montrose Register of Sasines, vol. 1637-1656, p. 125).

Dr Robert Strachan, physician in Montrose, had a younger son, John. The precise date of his birth is unknown. On the 24th September 1656, he was admitted schoolmaster of Montrose, by the town council of that burgh. The minute of his appointment runs thus:

"*Vigesimo quarto Septembres* 1656.—This day the counsall did admit and resave Mr Johne Strathauchane, sone lawfull to Dr Robert Strachane, to be scoole maister of this burghe ad culpam, and have conditioned and permitted to pay to him yeirlie, sevinscor merkis Scottes money quarterlie, to witt at Candilmas, Ruidday, Lambes, and Alhallawes, beginning the first quarteris payment thairoff at Candilmas nextocome, and so furthe quarterlie thaireftir, and that by and attour the ordinar quarter payment, payed by the scollaris and other casualties belonging to the scoolmaister; and the said Mr John Strachane promessis to remaine five yeiris with the scoole and during that space to attend the same deligentlie, and not goe to the presbitrie, nor exercise, nor tak himsellf to any other studies."

Prior to August 1659, Mr John Strachan was admitted to the parochial charge of Strachan, Kincardineshire. The proceedings in relation to the appointment of his successor, in the office of schoolmaster of Montrose, are in the records of the town council detailed thus:

"*Sexto Augusti* 1659.—The counsaill condiscend that Mr James Wishart sal be admitted to be Mr. of the Grammar Scoole of this burghe, efter tryall being fund qualified, and the counsall appoynts the Clerk to goe to the presbitrie for this effect, this next presbitrie day.

"*Vltimo Augusti* 1659.—This day the counsall have admitted Mr James Wishart to be scoolmaister of this burghe, ad culpam, and have permitted and conditioned to pay to him yeirlie during his service, sevenscor merks Scottes money, at the four quarteris of the yeir, to witt Candlemes, Ruidday, Lambes, and Hallamas, beginning the first quarteris payment thairoff at Lambes last bypast, and that by and attour his ordinar quarter payment, payed by the scolleris and other casualties belonging to the scoolmaister; and the said Mr James promitts and obliges him to attend the scoole carefullie and diligentlie, and not to tak himsellf to any other imployment that may anywayis avert him from his charge" (Montrose Burgh Records).

On the 14th August 1678, Mr John Strachan, minister of Strachan, obtained sasine of a tenement at Montrose, which he had acquired from Robert Jamieson, his sister's son (Montrose Register of Sasines, vol. 1670-1687, fol. 76). He married first, Beatrice, third daughter of David Strachan, Bishop of Brechin, who died in June 1668, leaving a son Robert, and a daughter, Jean; in her will she nominated her husband as her executor (Com. Register of Brechin). He married, secondly, in 1669, Margaret Speid (Scott's Fasti Eccl. Scot., vol. iii., p. 541; Montrose Register of Sasines, vol. 1686-1699, fol. 138). Of this marriage were

Memorials of the Families of Strachan and Wise. 77

born three sons and one daughter. Mr John Strachan died between the 28th January and 26th February 1701. In his will dated at Strachan, 20th January 1701, he bequeaths to his daughter Elizabeth £1000, due by Sir Thomas Burnett of Leys, and names his sons "James, Mr Robert, Mr Alexander, and John" as legatees (Scott's Fasti Eccl. Scot., vol. iii., p. 541; Montrose Register of Sasines, vol. 1686-1699, fol. 138; Will of Mr John Strachan, in Com. Register of Brechin).

Robert Strachan, eldest son of Mr John Strachan, minister of Strachan, became Rector of the Grammar School of Montrose. He married Elizabeth, daughter of Mr James Wishart, whom he succeeded as Rector of the Grammar School in 1683, and sister of Mr William Wishart, minister of Wamfray, by whom he had four sons and three daughters: John, baptized 19th September 1689, died July 1694; James, baptized 27th July 1696, died young; Robert, baptized 6th February 1698; David, baptized 22d February 1700 (Montrose Parish Registers). David was, on the 26th April 1759, served heir to his relative, Charles Strachan, Deputy-Governor of Guernsey. The proceedings in the service are as follow:

"At Montrose the twenty-sixth day of April, one thousand seven hundred and fifty-nine years. Which day, in presence of Thomas Christie, one of the present bailies of the said burgh sitting in judgment in a judicial fenced court, holden by him within the new council house thereof, compeared Charles Thomson, Writer in Montrose, as procurator for David Strachan, eldest lawful son of the deceased Mr Robert Strachan, late rector of the Grammar School of Montrose, who was the only son procreat betwixt umquhil Mr John Strachan sometime minister of the Gospel at Strachan, and [Beatrice] Strachan, his spouse, who was lawful daughter of the deceast [David] Strachan, bishop of Brechin, and produced a brieve furth of his majesties chancery, directed to the provost and baillies of Montrose, for serving the said David Strachan as nearest and lawful heir to the deceased Charles Strachan, late Deputy Governor of the island of Guernsey, who was lawful son of umquhil [James] Strachan, commissary of Brechin, who was lawful son of the said [David] Strachan, bishop of Brechin; together with the said magistrates their precept directed to the officers of the said burgh for proclaiming the said brieve, with an execution on the back thereof, under the hand of John Wright, officer, bearing that upon the sixth day of April instant, being Friday, the ordinary mercat day of this burgh, he duly proclaimed the said brieve in time of public mercat, to be served before the magistrates foresaid this day, and all persons having or pretending to have interest to have been lawfully summoned by the officer foresaid, and being this day thrice publickly called at the bar by an officer as use is, and none appearing to object anything to the contrary, the said Charles Thomson, procurator foresaid, protested *contra omnes mortales non comparentes;* and desired the said brieve might be remitted to the knowledge of an Inquest, which protestation the baillie admitted, and remitted the said Brieve to the Inquest following, viz.,

Geo. Ross, late provost.	Alexander Strachan, of Tarrie.
Jas. Dall, senr., shoemr.	William Ouchterlony, shipmaster.
Thomas Gairdner, wright.	Dr John Milne, physician.
Wm. Jamieson, wright.	Mr Pat. Simpson, merchant.
John Ritchie, merchant.	Da. Low, gunsmith.
	Da. Buchanan, shoemaker.
	Lieut. James Strachan.
	Thomas Davidson, merchant.
	Mr Wm. Petrie, Dr. of the Grammar School.
	James Donaldson, merchant.

" Which persons of Inquest having been solemnly sworn and admitted, and having by a plurality of votes elected the said Dr John Milne to be their chancellor, the said Charles Thomson presented to them the following claim :—' Good men of Inquest, I, the before-named David Strachan, eldest lawful son of the deceased Mr Robert Strachan, late rector of the Grammar School of Montrose, who was the only son procreat betwixt umquhill Mr John Strachan and [Beatrice] Strachan, his spouse, who was lawful daughter of the deceased [David] Strachan, bishop of Brechin, say unto your wisdoms, that my grand-uncle's son, the deceased Charles Strachan, late deputy-governor of the Island of Guernsey, who was lawful son of the deceased [James] Strachan, commissary of Brechin, who was lawful son of the said deceased [David] Strachan, bishop of Brechin, died at the faith and peace of our sovereign Lord now reigning, and that I am nearest and lawful heir to the said Charles Strachan, and this I desire may be retoured under most part of your wisdoms' seals.

'(Signed) DAVID STRACHAN.'

" For proving the propinquity of blood, the said Lieutenant James Strachan, one of the members of the Inquest, depones that he was acquainted with the deceased Mr Robert Strachan, late rector of the Grammar School of Montrose, father to the above-named David Strachan, and knows that the said Mr Robert Strachan was habit and repute to be lawful son procreat betwixt Mr John Strachan, minister of Strachan, and [Beatrice] Strachan, his first spouse, who was daughter to David Strachan, bishop of Brechin. *Causa scientiæ,* the deponent's own father Mr George Strachan was also a son of the said Mr John Strachan, by his second wife, and he has often heard and had occasion to converse with persons who had

occasion to know that the said Mr Robert Strachan was a son of Mr John Strachan's by his first wife, Bishop Strachan's daughter. This is truth as he shall answer to God.
(Signed)   J. STRACHAN.

"The before-named Alexander Strachan of Tarrie, another member of the Inquest, depones that he was well acquainted with the now deceased Mr Robert Strachan, father to the before-named David Strachan the petitioner, and he also knew the deceased Mr John Strachan, minister at Strachan, and that the said Mr Robert Strachan was habit and repute to be the said Mr John Strachan's son by his first wife, who was a daughter of umquhill David Strachan, bishop of Brechin. Depones that he was particularly well acquainted with the before-named umqnhill Charles Strachan, late deputy-governor of the Island of Guernsey, and that he was alwise habit and repute to be the lawful son of the deceased [James] Strachan, commissary of Brechin, who was son to the said umquhill David Strachan, bishop there. *Causa scientiæ*, he has often heard from persons who had occasion to know it, and this is truth as he shall answer to God.   (Signed)   ALEXR. STRACHAN.

"For further instructing the said David Strachan's propinquity of blood to the said Charles Strachan, the before-named Charles Thomson, produced letters of supplement under his majesties signet, at David Strachan's instances against witnesses, with sundry executions thereof, and particularly one against Margaret Ross after designed, and craved she might be called and examined, and she was accordingly called.
(Signed)   DAVID STRACHAN.

"Compeared the said Margaret Ross, relict of the deceast Mr David Rose, minister of the gospel at Woodside, who being solemnly sworn and interrogated, depones, that she has often heard from her own mother, who was a daughter of the before-named Mr John Strachan, minister of Strachan, by his second wife, that Mr Robert Strachan, late rector of the Grammar School of Montrose, was the only son procreat betwixt the said Mr John Strachan and [Beatrice] Strachan, his first wife, who was the daughter of the before-named Mr David Strachan, bishop of Brechin, and that she has also heard it from her own mother, that [James] Strachan, commissary of Brechin, was son to the said Mr David Strachan, bishop there, and that the before-named Charles Strachan was son to the said Commissary Strachan. All this is truth as she shall answer to God.   (Signed)   MARGARET ROSE.

"As also compeared Margaret Wood, relict of John Wallace, late Convener of the Trades of Arbroath. Witness also lawfully cited by virtue of the foresaid letters of supplement, who being solemnly sworn and interrogat, depones that the deceased Mr Robert Strachan, late rector of the Grammar School of Montrose, father to the said David Strachan, was alwise habit and repute to be a full cousin-german to the before-named Charles Strachan, late deputy-governor of the Island of Guernsey, being both of them habit and repute to be grandchildren to Bishop Strachan, bishop of Brechin. This she has often had occasion to hear, for she was acquainted with the said Charles Strachan when he was a boy, and the deponent herself was well acquainted with the now deceased Mary Mathew, who was also a grandchild of Bishop Strachan's, and she has heard her frequently talking of their relation betwixt the said Mr Robert Strachan and Charles Strachan. This is truth as she shall answer to God.

(Signed) M. WOOD.

"The persons of Inquest foresaid, having considered the foresaid Brieve, Execution thereof, and claim and probation adduced for instructing the same, they all in one voice by the said doctor John Milne, chancellor, chosen by them for that effect, serve the said David Strachan heir to the said deceased Charles Strachan, his grand-uncle's son, in general, and ordain him to be retoured under most part of their seals.

(Signed) JOHN MILNE, Ch.

"*Return general of David Strachan, to the Son of his Great Grand-Uncle.*

(Translated from the Latin.)

"This Inquisition was made in the Town Hall of the Borough of Montrose, on the 26th day of the month of April A.D. 1759, in presence of Thomas Christie, one of the bailies of said borough, by these honest and loyal subjects subscribed, to wit: Alexander Strachan of Tarrie, native of Montrose; George Ross, lately provost of said borough; John Milne, doctor of medicine there; John Ritchie, Mr Patrick Simpson, Thomas Davidson, and James Donaldson, merchants there; William Ouchterlony, skipper there; James Strachan, native there, lately lieutenant H.M. ship Cambridge; Mr William Petrie, assistant teacher of the Grammar School there; James Dall, senior, and David Buchanan, shoemakers there; Thomas Gairdner and William Jamieson, carpenters there; and David Low, blacksmith there. Who being sworn, declare (on their solemn oath) that the late Charles Strachan, lately deputy-governor of the Island of Guernsey, who was son of [James] Strachan, commissary of Brechin, who was son of Mr David Strachan, bishop of Brechin, who was son of the great grand-uncle of David Strachan, bearer of these presents, who was eldest legitimate son of Mr Robert Strachan, lately rector of the Grammar School of Montrose, who was sole son begot by Mr John Strachan, sometime minister of the gospel at Strachan, and of [Beatrice] Strachan, his first wife, who was daughter of the said deceased David Strachan, bishop of Brechin, died in peace, and loyalty to our king now reigning; and that the said David Strachan is lawful and nearest heir of said late Charles Strachan, son of his great grand-uncle. The rest of the other clauses of the brieve hereinafter served, remain because nothing further is therein contained in the petition so far completed.

"In witness whereof, the common seal of said borough is appended to these presents, the brieve royal included, by the hand of William Speid of said borough, and in the premises of Town-Clerk aforesaid; and the seals of certain of those who were present at the said inquisition; in the year, day, and month, and place afore mentioned" (From Original Service in the Town-Clerk's Office, Montrose).

Of the three daughters of Robert Strachan, Rector of the Grammar School of Montrose, Helen, the eldest, was baptized 18th July 1691;

Margaret, the second daughter, was baptized 16th February 1693; and Jean, the third daughter, was baptized 20th March 1695 (Montrose Parish Register). Robert Strachan and his wife died prior to the 6th September 1707 (Montrose Register of Sasines, vol. 1703-1720, fols. 21 and 22, 174 and 185).

George Strachan is described as eldest son of Mr John Strachan, minister at Strachan, by his second wife Margaret Speid, in a sasine dated 8th June 1696 (Montrose Register of Sasines, vol. 1686-1699, fol. 138). He was, on the 17th June 1702, infeft in a tenement, to which he had succeeded on the death of his father. He married Catherine, daughter of —— Turnbull of Smiddyhill, by whom he had two sons, John and James, and a daughter, Margaret. Margaret, only daughter of George Strachan, married, in 1727, Alexander Wyse of Lunan, with issue (see postea).

John Strachan, elder son of George Strachan, died April 1705 (Montrose Parish Register). James, the second son (Inquest of Service of David Strachan, April 1759, in town clerk's office, Montrose), became a lieutenant in the Royal Navy. He served on board H.M. ship the "Cambridge," and on retiring from active service, resided first in London, and afterwards in Montrose. On the 1st June 1752, he obtained sasine of a tenement on the east side of Murray Street, Montrose (Montrose Register of Sasines, vol. 1742-1752, fol. 181). He married Catherine, daughter of James Donaldson, merchant in Montrose, and relict of James Mudie, shipmaster there; and on the 10th August 1756, obtained sasine of a tenement in Montrose, belonging to his wife, in implement of his marriage-contract, dated 8th June 1750 (Burgh Register of Sasines, vol. 1755-1761, fol. 69).

Lieutenant James Strachan obtained sasine of a bond on a tenement in Montrose, 9th September 1763, and in an annual rent on a portion of ground in that burgh, 26th November 1764. He and his wife Catherine Donaldson, had sasine of a tenement in Murray Street, Montrose, on the 1st August 1775 (Montrose Register of Sasines, vol. 1761-1768, and vol. 1773-1777). Mrs Catherine Strachan died on the 11th March 1782, aged sixty-three; Lieutenant Strachan on the 9th September 1794, aged ninety-three. A tombstone in the parish churchyard of Montrose, commemorating Lieutenant James Strachan, his wife, and infant daughter, is sculptured with the Thornton shield, bearing a stag tripping *or*, attired and unguled *or*, with the family motto, "Non timeo sed careo." The legend is as follows:

"Here lies Margaret Strachan, daughter to Lieutenant James Strachan, of the Royal Navy, who died the 12th day of December 1761, aged 8 years. Also Catherine Donaldson, his spouse, who died the 11th day of March 1782, aged 63 years. And the said Lieutenant James Strachan, who died the 9th day of September 1794, aged 93 years."[1]

Lieutenant James Strachan had by his wife, Catherine Donaldson, a son, John, and a daughter, Margaret. The latter died on the 12th December 1761, aged eight years (Tombstone in Montrose Churchyard).

John Strachan was born on the 22d March 1751 (Tombstone Inscription). On the 12th March 1792, he had sasine on a disposition by his father of a tenement in Montrose, and on the 26th January 1795, he received cognition as "lawful son and heir of Lieutenant James Strachan, deceased," with sasine in certain tenements in Montrose which had belonged to his father (Montrose Register of Sasines, vol. 1789-1792, fols. 221, 237). After residing some time at Woodside, near Montrose, he purchased the estate of Cliffden, near Teignmouth, Devonshire. Having adopted proceedings in the Scottish Court of Chancery for maintaining his claim to the baronetcy of Thornton, he was, on the 10th August 1840,

---

[1] In the Mortality Register of Montrose is the following entry: "1794, Sep. 13, Lieut. James Strachan, buried, B. M." [Best Mortcloth].

served by a jury in the Burgh Court of the Canongate, " nearest and legitimate heir-male in general of umquhile John Strachan of Monboddo, his great-great-great-great-grandfather." Further services on his behalf were effected on the 25th October 1841, by which he was found " sole lawful son of the deceased James Strachan, lieutenant, sometime of the Royal Navy, who was the only lawful son of the deceased George Strachan, Esq., sometime merchant in Montrose, who was lawful son of the deceased John Strachan, sometime minister of Strachan." He was at the same time served " nearest of blood and lawful heir-male in general of umquhile Sir Alexander Strachan of Thornton [created a baronet on 28th of May 1625], his cousin by the father's side" (Services in Chancery).

Served heir-male of his House, Mr John Strachan of Cliffden thereafter became known by the style and title of Sir John Strachan, Bart. of Thornton. He died at Cliffden, East Teignmouth, on the 9th June 1844. On his tombstone he is celebrated as " beloved and respected for his many eminent virtues, through a long and useful life, his pure and unaffected piety, and the warm benevolence of his heart." Sir John married Elizabeth, daughter of David Hunter, Esq. of Blackness, Forfarshire, by whom he was father of two sons and three daughters.

James Graham, the younger son, was born 3d January 1789. He held an appointment in the East India Civil Service, Bombay, and died at Malacca, unmarried, in September 1813 (Tombstone Inscription).

John, elder son of Sir John Strachan, Bart., was born in 1784. He succeeded to the baronetcy of Thornton on the death of his father in June 1844. On his tombstone at East Teignmouth is the following inscription :

" Sacred to the memory of Sir John Strachan, Bart. of Thornton, Scotland, and of Cliffden in this parish, who, after a long and painful illness, departed this life on the 28th day of January 1854, in the 70th year of his age. ' Blessed are the dead which die in the Lord.' "

Sir John Strachan, Bart., second of Cliffden, married Mary Ann, daughter of Isaac Elton, Esq. of White Staunton, Somersetshire; she died at East Teignmouth, s.p.

Catherine, eldest daughter of Sir John Strachan, Bart., and Elizabeth Hunter, married John Cave, Esq. of Brentry, Gloucestershire; she died, s.p., about the year 1872 at Portishead, Bristol.

Jane Elizabeth, youngest daughter of Sir John Strachan, Bart., and Elizabeth Hunter, was born on the 26th March 1786, and died at Cliffden, unmarried, 7th July 1817 (Tombstone Inscription).

Amelia, second daughter of Sir John Strachan, Bart., and Elizabeth Hunter, was born in 1781. She married the Rev. William Page Richards, D.C.L., Rector of Stoke Abbot, Dorsetshire, and incumbent of East Teignmouth, who died 2d April 1861, aged eighty-eight (Tombstone Inscription). Mrs Amelia Richards or Strachan died on the 9th February 1852, aged seventy-one (Tombstone Inscription). Of the marriage of the Rev. Dr Richards and Amelia Strachan, were born three daughters. Amelia Frances, eldest daughter, is unmarried. Elizabeth Jane, the second daughter, married, 1st June 1843, Augustus Maitland, fourth son of Sir Alexander Charles Maitland, Bart. of Cliftonhall, who died 26th January 1855. On the death of her maternal uncle, Sir John Strachan, Bart., in 1854, Mrs Maitland assumed the name of Strachan. She has four sons—Augustus Alexander William John, Alexander Charles Richards, William James, and Frederick Henry. By his will, dated 29th June 1848, Sir John Strachan, Bart., who died in 1854, bequeathed his estate of Cliffden to Augustus Alexander William John, described as "eldest son of his niece, Elizabeth Jane Richards, and her husband, Augustus Maitland," the testator enjoining the legatee to use the surname and arms of Strachan of Thornton only.

Catherine Augusta, the third daughter, married Colonel John Whitehead Pearl of Trenython, Cornwall. Of this marriage have been born four daughters, Catherine Matilda, Emily, Alice, and Ada. Emily, second daughter, married Captain George Purcell, R.N.; he died in 1873. Alice, third daughter, married the Rev. Edward K. Kendall, incumbent of St Mark's, Notting Hill, London. Ada, fourth daughter, married Joseph T. Treffry, Esq.

We now return to David, younger son of James Strachan of Monboddo, who died on the 10th July 1614. He is named along with his elder brother Robert (afterwards Dr Robert Strachan, physician in Montrose), in his father's will (Com. Reg. of St Andrews, 20th April 1615). On the 13th November 1616, he had the grant of a tenement in Montrose from his nephew, James Strachan of Monboddo (see *supra*). By his father's will, the care of his upbringing was entrusted to Alexander, afterwards Sir Alexander Strachan, Bart. of Thornton, and John Strachan of Phesdo, that baronet's uncle.[1] He entered as a student the University of Edinburgh, and there graduated 27th July 1622. In 1630, on the presentation of Charles I., he was ordained minister of Fettercairn. He was a member of the Commissions of Assembly 1645, 1647, and 1648. On the 4th February 1646, he petitioned Parliament, craving repayment of certain losses. He was named by Parliament, 23d February 1661, one of the commissioners for visiting the University of Aberdeen (Fasti Eccl. Scot., vol. iii., p. 866). Through the influence of his relative, the Earl of Middleton, he was appointed Bishop of Brechin in 1662. With Mr John Strachan, the archdeacon, he concurred in granting a portion of land to the Hospital of Brechin on the 11th April 1667 (Burgh Records of Brechin). A placard in the session-house at Brechin bears that in 1665

---

[1] The laird of Thornton and John Strachan of Phesdo were about the same time appointed overseers in charge of David Strachan in Burartoun, parish of Marykirk, a minor (Commissariat Register of St Andrews, June 27, 1621).

he presented the orlodge (clock) to the steeple. He died on the 9th October 1671 (Brechin Presbytery Records). His remains were interred in the cathedral of Brechin in front of the pulpit (Black's History of Brechin, p. 318). His funeral sermon was preached on the 12th October by Mr William Peirson, minister of Dunfermline (Fasti Eccl. Scot.).

Bishop Strachan was twice married. By his first wife, Margaret Henderson, he was father of two sons, David and James, and four daughters, Beatrice, Christian, Mary, and Margaret. He married, secondly, Anna, daughter of Captain David Barclay of Mathers, and sister of Colonel David Barclay of Urie, a widow. The marriage-contract is dated at Aberluthnot (Marykirk), the 21st May 1649 (Genealogical Account of Barclays of Urie, Lond. 1812, pp. 23, 24). The will of Bishop Strachan, executed on the 8th October 1671, the day preceding his decease, proceeds thus :

"I, Dauid, be the mercie off God, Bishop off Brechine, being at present under distemper of bodie, but perfyt in memoire and jugment, and taking to my consideratione that all men ar mortall, and the tyme off death uncertane, I doe herfor make my will and testament as followis : In the first place, I doe comitt my soule to God, being assured to be saved by the merits of Jesus Chryst my Saviour ; and, for ordoring off my worldlie affairs and to prevent any debaitt or question tha tmay aryse betwixt my dear and loving wyff, Anna Barclay, and my children, or my children amongst themselffes, I doe in the first place declare that it is my will, lykas with consent off Mr Daniel Strachan, my eldest sone, and James Strachan, my second sone, I will and ordain that my said dear and loving wyff shall have her lyfrent right during all the dayes off her lyftyme, off all and sundrie whatsoever sownes of money is dew and restand awand and belouging to me either by bond, tiket, compt, or any other maner of way ; as also her vse during her said lyftyme, of all and heall the plenishing within and belonging to our house and familie, on this express condition, that her forsaid lyfrent provision shall be in full compleit satisfaction of what can accresh, fall, and belong to my said wyff, be vertew of our contract of mariage, or quhilk could fall to her as tere or third of movables, or be any other richt or titill efter my deceiss ; and wills her to discharge my execeutor eftirnamed theroff, reserving her lyfrent : And when it pleases God to call her by death, it is also my will and desyre that shee keip the plenishing off our house intire, and not to dispose, neither suffer the same to be wronged or rifled, except to give or leave a litill portion theroff to her dauchter, and to Anna Hoy her grandchyld : And morover the forsaid lyfrent richt off what belongs to me, and her lyfrent vse off the plenishing off the house is not only on the conditions forsaid, but also on this condition, that shee will entertain the said James Strachan my sone, and Margaret Strachan my daughter, honestlie during all the dayes of my said wyff her lyftyme, and that shee take that inspection over them as becomes a parent, and keip them with her in familie, recomending alway to my said wyff, that she will remember according to her promise (to me) that at her death she wold leave to me or my children the halff off that sex thousand merks, dew to her restand be my Lord Midlton: And I heirby injoyne, comand, and ordain my whole children, as they respect me, to be dutiefull and respective of my said wyff during her lyftyme : And further, I leave and dispone to the said Master Dauid Strachan, minister at Moutrose, my sone, the whole books belonging and apertening to me, as also the sowme of ane thousand merks off that sowme of two thousand merks dew to me be the laird of Balyordie ; and the other sowme off ane thousand merks theroff, I leave and dispone to the said Margaret Strachan, my dauchter ; and I leave and dispone to Grissell Strachan, now wyff to Mr Robert ———, the sowme of sex hundereth merkes ; and I leave and dispone to the children off Mr John Mathie and Marie Strachan his spous, the sowme off sex hundereth merkes ; and I leave to Jean Strachan, my grandchyld, dauchter to Mr John Strachan, minister att Strachan, two hundereth merkes ; and to the rest off his children, who ar my oyes, the sowme of other two hundereth merkes, provyding alway that if it pleass God to call the said Margaret Strachan, my dauchter, and the children off the said Mr John Strachan, without lawfull children off ther own bodie, her seuerall legacies forsaid to returne full and belong to the saidis Mr Dauid Strachan and James Strachan, my sones, equallie betuixt them : And I leave and dispone the sowme of dew to me be John Toddie to   ; and the rest off my goods, gear, debt, and sowmes off money belonging, or that shall be belonging to me, I leave and dispone the samen to James Strachan, my laufull sone, whom I heirby nominatt and constitut as my executor and vniversall legator, except the legacies forsaid ; and ordaines him to pay and satisfie what small debts I am restand to anie persone, and to secure not onlie what sowmes ar dew to me on bond, but also what the yeirs rent and bygon rests off the bishoprik comes to, and make the same als soon as is possible, in a stok for the lyfrent vse of my said wyff, and for the severall legators forsaid, and his owne vse and behoove eftir her deceis, provyding he be not lyable to compt for more then he receaves, and what expenses he shall be att to be alloued to him proportionalie to evrie ones benifit : And further, I will and ordain my said executor to improve himself for obtaining payment of the whole or a part off that money dew to me as bishop of Brechin, out off the excheiquer ; and what he receaves, to be equallie devydit (eftir his expens is alloued) amongst the said Mr Dauid, James, and Margaret Strachans ; and, if he obtain anie considerable sowme, to help the rest of the legators forsaid at his discretion : Finallie, I doe comitt and recomend my said wyff and children to God, etc.—In witness quheroff, I have, with consent off my said wyff and children present agreeing tharto, subscrybit thir presents. Wreatine be Johne Spence, clerke off Brechine, at Brechine the eight day off October 1671, befor thir witneses, Doctor James Dixon, Mr Laurens Skinner, merchant at Brechin, and Alex^{r.} Strachan, my servant.

Thus subscribed in Latin: "By command of the said David, bishop of Brechin, he being unable to write, as he asserted, by reason of illness, I, John Spence, notary public, subscribe.

"J. Spence, N.P.

"INVENTORY of the goods, gear, etc., pertaining to the deceased reverend father in God, David, bishop of Brechin, and possessed in common betwixt him and Anna Barklay, his spouse, the time of his decease, who deceased in the month of October 1671; made and given up by himself, touching the nomination of his executor and disposition of his goods and gear; and the Inventory is made and given up by James Strachan, his lawful son, and executor nominated by the said defunct. The plenishing of the house is given up by the said executor as worth £66, 13s. 4d. The sum of the debts is £7115, 8s. The sum of the Inventory and debts is £7182, 1s. 4d." (Com. Reg. of Brechin).

Of his four daughters, Margaret seems to have died unmarried; Christian married Mr Robert ———; Mary married Mr John Mathie; and Beatrice married Mr John Strachan, minister of Strachan; she died in June 1668, leaving a son, Robert,[1] and a daughter, Jean. In her will, Mrs Beatrice Strachan nominated her husband as her executor (Commissariat Register of Brechin).

Of Bishop Strachan's two sons, James, the younger, became Commissary of Brechin. He married his cousin, Barbara Henderson, and died in April 1685, leaving two sons, Laurence, who died unmarried, and Charles, and a daughter, Anne. His will, recorded in the Commissariat Register of Brechin, embraces these particulars: Among the debts due to him is a bond for £253, 6s. 8d., by Andro Wood of Balgeno "to vmquhille David, Bishop of Brechin, father to the defunct," to which he had right as executor; also a bond for £30, 13s. 4d., by James Strachan of Kirktoun of Lethintie (Lethendy), to Bishop Strachan, dated 1st August 1661; and a bond by Patrick, Earl of Strathmore, to the bishop for £1333, 6s. 8d., dated 10th April 1672. In his will he provides for his relict, in liferent, whatever should remain after payment of expenses; and which, after her death, should fall to Anne, Laurence, and Charles Strachan, his children, equally. He recommends his "honorable freinds" the lairds of Balnamoon and Phinheavin to assist his relict with their advice. The will is dated at Brechin on the 1st April 1685.

[1] For an account of Robert Strachan, see *supra*.

Charles Strachan was baptized on the 25th September 1683 (Baptismal Register of Brechin). He became Deputy-Governor of the island of Guernsey, and died some time prior to the 26th April 1759, when David Strachan, son of Mr Robert Strachan, rector of the Grammar School of Montrose, was by a jury served as his nearest and lawful heir in general (Record of Services of Heirs, Town Clerk's Office, Montrose).

David, elder son of Bishop Strachan, studied at the University of St Andrews, and in 1662 was ordained minister of the first charge, Montrose. He died 2d July 1672 in his thirty-third year (Fasti Eccl. Scot., vol. iii., p. 844). He was father of two sons, James, baptized 30th May 1666, and David, baptized 15th July 1668, and a daughter, Margaret, baptized 14th June 1663, died May 1676 (Montrose Parish Register). The male line of David, Bishop of Brechin,[1] is extinct.

At a date considerably anterior to the year 1614, when Dr Robert Strachan established his residence at Montrose, a branch of the House of Strachan settled as merchants in that place. Early in the seventeenth century, a member of this branch invested the proceeds of successful merchandise in the estate of Tarrie, near Arbroath, which he transmitted to his descendants. Patrick Strachan, described as son of

---

[1] From a remote branch of the House of Strachan of Thornton, sprung other two bishops. John Strachan, Bishop of Brechin, was born in 1719, on the farm of Redford in the parish of Garvock, Kincardineshire. Obtaining orders in the Episcopal Church, he ministered to a small congregation at Redmon, near Laurencekirk, and aided his revenues by renting the small farm of Bush of Lauriston in the vicinity. He was afterwards incumbent of the Episcopal church, Dundee, and Bishop of Brechin. He died unmarried on the 2d February 1810, at the age of ninety-one (Tombstone Inscription, Dundee). John Strachan, Bishop of Toronto, was a native of Aberdeenshire. Born about the year 1774, he studied at the Universities of Aberdeen and St Andrews. He was parochial schoolmaster, first at Dunino, and afterwards at Kettle, Fifeshire. Proceeding to Upper Canada, in 1799, he engaged in tuition. Obtaining orders, he was in 1812 appointed to a charge in Toronto; he was appointed bishop of that diocese in 1839. A zealous promoter of education, Bishop Strachan founded the University of King's College, Canada. He died about the year 1866 at a venerable age.

the late Alexander Strachan in Nether Tarrie, parish of St Vigeans, near Arbroath, died in February 1620. In his will, which was confirmed on the 24th June of the same year, his executors are his brothers and sisters,—viz., David Strachan in Newtoun, Walter Strachan in Nether Tarrie, Janet, spouse of Charles Keany in Arbroath, and Isabel, spouse of John Dickson there (Com. Reg. of St Andrews, vol. vii.). Alexander Strachan, styled " in South Tarrie, parish of St Vigeans," died on the 9th June 1624, leaving a widow, Margaret Futhie, and six sons—Alexander, John, Henry, Andrew, William, and James, and a daughter, Isabell (Com. Reg. of St Andrews, vol. viii.). On the 12th June 1729, Alexander Strachan of Tarrie, " merchant in Montrose," obtained sasine on a disposition by George Beattie of a tenement in Murray Street, Montrose (Montrose Reg. of Sasines, vol. 1727-1742, fol. 34). Alexander Strachan of Tarrie was in 1759 one of the inquest for serving David Strachan heir to his relative, Charles Strachan, Governor of Guernsey, and was also a witness in the service (see *supra*). Having married Elizabeth, daughter of Sir David Carnegie of Pitarrow, a descendant of the first Earl of Southesk, he had two sons, David and Alexander, and two daughters, Jean and Elizabeth. Both the sons died unmarried. Alexander Strachan died in February 1761, and was succeeded in the estate of Tarrie by his daughter Jean, who married Thomas Rennie, younger son of Patrick Rennie of Usan, near Montrose. Of this marriage the elder son was Alexander Strachan, who, on the death of his mother, succeeded to the family estate. He married, first, Miss Stephen, heiress of Letham, and secondly, in 1807, Elizabeth, daughter of William Ford of Montrose. Having died without issue, Alexander Strachan was succeeded by his brother, Thomas Rennie, Writer to the Signet, who took the name of Strachan. This gentleman married Harriet Moyes; he died without issue, 20th October 1823.

Consequent on an entail executed by Thomas Rennie Strachan in 1812, the estate of Tarrie is now the property of John Carnegie, second son of Sir David Carnegie, fourth baronet of Southesk. To his patronymic he has prefixed the names of Rennie Strachan. Captain Rennie Strachan Carnegie was born at Kinnaird on the 19th June 1802. He married 7th September 1848, Elizabeth Susan, daughter of Lieutenant-Colonel John Grey of Backsworth, Northumberland, and has a son, Claud Cathcart, born 9th December 1849 (Fraser's Earls of Southesk; Burke's Landed Gentry).

Sixty years after the creation of the baronetcy of Strachan of Thornton, a second baronetcy was granted to a scion of that ancient House. Thomas Strachan, a descendant of the old barons of Thornton, was a soldier of fortune, and joined the army of Leopold I., Emperor of Germany. From James VII., in 1685, he received a patent of baronetcy. That instrument, rendered into English, proceeds thus:

"JAMES, by the grace of God, King of Great Britain, France, and Ireland, and Defender of the Faith, etc. Since we, reflecting in our own royal mind that all titles of honour and dignity within these our dominions flow forth from us solely as fountainhead and spring, towards those of our subjects who deserve well of us; and finding, moreover, the loyalty, worth, dignity, and great merits of Thomas Strachan, our beloved subject, at present serving in the wars under his Imperial Majesty, to be sufficiently established, and resolving to bestow upon him, and his heirs after him, some lasting token of our royal favour, not only on account of his own good qualities, but also that he is sprung from the House of Thornton, one of the oldest and most loyal among the very many old and loyal families of this our realm of Scotland: by which House and others his ancestors foresaid, very many excellent services were rendered to many of our illustrious progenitors of blessed memory: and further, we of our kindness, being inclined not only to encourage our well-deserving servants dwelling in these our dominions, but also those of them who are travelling among foreign nations (whose conduct may render them worthy): Know ye, therefore, that of our perfect knowledge, power, and privilege, we have given, granted, and conferred, and, by the tenor of these presents, do give, grant, and confer upon our foresaid loyal and well-beloved subject, Thomas Strachan and the heirs-male of his body, the title, dignity, rank, and honour of Knight-Baronet; and we accordingly ordain that he and the aforesaids shall possess and enjoy the said title, together with the precedence, priority, and all other privileges and honours due to knights-baronets, by all statute acts, diplomas, or customs whatever, in these our dominions, but especially in all sessions, conventions, and other assemblies whatever, public or private, in our said realm: and further, we ordain that the wives and children of the said Thomas Strachan and his heirs, shall equally have and possess priority and precedence due to wives, heirs, and others, children of knights-baronets. And furthermore, generally by these presents, and by all solemn rites and ceremonies formerly in use in such cases, we decree and order the Lyon King at Arms and his brother heralds henceforth to give and to grant such arms, or additions to existent arms, due to him and to his House, as seem proper and convenient on this occasion. In witness whereof we have ordered our great seal to be appended to these presents. At our Court of Whitehall, the 8th day of May 1685" (Reg. Mag. Sig., lib. lxx., No. 31).

Described in the patent as "sprung from the House of Thornton," Thomas Strachan appears to have descended less remotely from the family of Strachan at Mureton in the neighbourhood of Laurencekirk. "Mr John Strachan of Muretoun" and "Thomas Strachan, his brother," are mentioned, the former as a cautioner, and the latter as one of the witnesses to an obligation by Sir Alexander Strachan of Thornton for borrowed money, dated 8th May 1638 (Register of Deeds, vol. 512).

Sir Thomas Strachan was, it is believed, son of Thomas Strachan, brother of the farmer at Mureton. To distinguish his baronetcy from that of the elder branch, he assumed the territorial designation "of Inchtuthill;" but this style was not adopted by his successors. According to a family pedigree deposited in the College of Arms by Admiral Sir Richard Strachan, Sir Thomas died without issue, when the baronetcy was assumed by Patrick, M.D., physician to Greenwich Hospital, his younger brother.

Dr Patrick Strachan married a daughter of Captain Gregory, R.N., and by her had two sons, John and Patrick. John succeeded his father in the baronetcy; he was a post-captain in the Navy, and in 1771 commanded H.M. ship "Oxford" of 70 guns, on board of which he served under Admiral Sir Robert Harland, and afterwards in India, where his brother Patrick was his first lieutenant. He married Elizabeth, daughter of Robert Lovelace, Esq., of Battersea Rise, Surrey, and died without issue, 26th December 1777.

Patrick Strachan, lieutenant, R.N., long resided at Greenwich. In 1759 he married Caroline, daughter of Captain John Pitman, R.N., by his wife, a sister of Stephen Mignan, an opulent merchant in Plymouth. He had two sons and two daughters. The daughters, Mary Caroline and Elizabeth Anne, both died unmarried. The younger son, Jervis Henry, an officer of marines, served under Admiral Rodney, and was killed in a sea engagement in 1780; he died unmarried.

Lieutenant Patrick Strachan died at New York, in 1776, having predeceased Sir John, his elder brother. His elder son, Richard John, succeeded to the baronetcy.

Richard John Strachan was born at Plymouth, on the 27th October 1760. Entering the navy on board the "Actaeon," he became, after the usual period of service, third lieutenant of the "Hero," 74 guns. After several changes, he attained the rank of post-captain in 1783. At the close of the American war, he obtained the command of the "Vesta," 28 guns, in which he conveyed reinforcements to Bombay. In command of the "Phœnix," a 36-gun frigate, he distinguished himself in protecting British trade, which would otherwise have suffered from interlopers under neutral colours. In November 1792, he attacked a French frigate, "La Resolue," which accompanied two coasting vessels, supposed to be laden with supplies for Tippoo Sultan, and compelled the French captain to strike his colours. On the outbreak of war with the French Republic, he joined, in the "Concord," 42 guns, the squadron under Sir John Borlase Warren, employed on the coast of France. In an engagement with a French squadron, fought on the 23d April 1794, he captured the "Engageante," after an action in which he evinced remarkable ardour and promptitude. In May 1795, while in command of the "Melampus,"

42 guns, he attacked off Cape Carterel thirteen French vessels, laden with military stores, escorted by an armed brig. Silencing the battery, he captured twelve of the vessels with the loss of only two British seamen.

In 1799 Sir Richard was promoted to the "Captain," 74 guns, in which, on the western coast of France, he distinguished himself, by crippling the enemy's trade, and keeping in check their armed cruisers. In command of the " Donegal," he captured the " Amphitrite," a Spanish ship of war, after a brisk and spirited engagement. While cruising off the Ferrol, in command of a squadron, in November 1805, he fell in with a division of French ships, which had escaped from the action at Trafalgar. After a decisive engagement, Sir Richard took possession of four line-of-battle ships, which he sent to Plymouth, to be added to the navy. In acknowledgment of his brilliant services, he was promoted to a flag, as Rear-Admiral of the Blue. By the Corporation of London he was voted a sword and the freedom of the city. In 1809 he was entrusted with the command of the great naval expedition to the Scheldt, the military force being placed under the command of the Earl of Chatham. The inactivity and incapacity of the military commander paralysed the efforts of his naval colleague, and rendered the enterprise a failure; while a strict investigation proved that the abortive character of the Walcheren expedition was in no respect due to the commander of the sea forces. In 1811 Sir Richard was advanced as Vice-Admiral, and on the 1st June 1812 was installed as a Knight of the Bath; he became Admiral in 1821. On his retirement he established his residence in Bryanston Square, London, where he died on the 3d February 1828, aged sixty-eight.

Sir Richard Strachan married, 28th April 1812, Miss Louisa Dillon. Of this marriage were born, 30th April 1813, a son who died young, and three daughters. Matilda Frances, the eldest daughter, born 31st May 1814, became the Countess Bertholdi; Charlotte Leopoldine, the second daughter, born 31st August 1815, married, 2d April 1837, Emmanuel, Count Zichny-Terraris, and died in India in November 1851; Sarah Louisa, the youngest daughter, is the Princess St Antimo. All have had issue. The eldest son of the Princess St Antimo is the Duke di Bagnaro, one of the wealthiest noblemen in Naples.

Lady Strachan married subsequently an Italian gentleman named Piccalillo, and having obtained a handsome legacy from Charles, third Marquis of Hertford, she purchased the title of Marchesa di Salza, and established her residence in a palace at Naples. She died there in 1868 at an advanced age.

Sir Richard Strachan executed his will on the 12th September 1816, to which he afterwards added six codicils, the last bearing date 31st January 1828. He bequeathed £10,467, 17s. 3d. in liferent to his sisters, Mary Caroline and Elizabeth Ann, spinsters, with the residue to his wife.

On the death of Sir Richard Strachan, the second baronetcy in the family of Strachan of Thornton lapsed by the extinction of heirs-male.

A representative of the ancient barons of Thornton in the female line is the head of the old Scottish family of Wise.

The family of Wyse or Wise is of Saxon origin. Oliver Wise, a powerful baron, held lands in the West of England prior to the Conquest. The present representative of the House in England is John Ayshford Wise, Esq. of Clayton Hall, in the county of Stafford, and of Hillesdon, county of Devon; he formerly represented Stafford in the House of Commons. Subsequent to the Conquest, a branch of the House effected a settlement in Scotland. In 1301, a member of the family commanded, under Robert the Bruce, the force by which the Lord of Lorne was defeated at Brander-awe, and again fought under Bruce's standard at the battle of Bannockburn in 1314. In a legal instrument, dated 10th October 1345, John Wyse is named as head of the priory of Pluscardine (Register of Moray, p. 169). In 1494-95, Adam Wise is mentioned as resident in or about Stirling. A descendant of the House appears in the middle of the seventeenth century as "Alexander Wysse of Mains of Thornton," in the parish of Laurencekirk, Kincardineshire. This gentleman had two sons. Alexander, the younger son, married Catherine Beattie of Laurencekirk, a relative of the celebrated Dr James Beattie, author of "The Minstrel." Of this marriage were born four daughters. Mary married James Don; Jean married William Jamieson; Isabella married David Low. James, eldest son of David and Isabella Low, possessed the estate of Laws, Berwickshire, and was father of the late David Low, Esq., Professor of Agriculture in the University of Edinburgh. Helen, eldest daughter (born 1707, died 1783), married, 24th July 1726, James Renny, and was mother of nine sons and four daughters. Henry, the third son, born 24th August 1738, married, first, Isabella Robinson, 14th September 1773, and secondly, in 1781, Mary Henderson; Jane, his second daughter, married, 18th April 1814, John Aberdein, Esq.; their eldest son is the present Francis Aberdein, Esq. of Keithock.

David, eldest son of Alexander Wysse of Mains of Thornton, married Margaret, eldest daughter of Alexander Keith, Esq. of Pitbuddo; their marriage-contract is dated at Montrose, 9th November 1681. Of this marriage were born two sons and three daughters. Margaret, the eldest daughter, married, first, James Lawson, Esq. of Whitesaugh, in the parish of St Cyrus; their marriage-contract is dated 26th July 1709; she married, secondly, —— Jamieson, Esq., in the parish of Lunan. Her remains are interred in the parish churchyard of Laurencekirk, by the grave of her first husband. She left issue.

Elizabeth, second daughter, married Arthur Shepherd, merchant, Laurencekirk; their contract is dated 8th April 1710. The eldest son of this marriage, Arthur Shepherd, was bred to the law, and became Sheriff of Kincardineshire. He married Margaret Keith, a relative of the Earl Marischal, and left issue.

Mary, third daughter of David Wysse and Margaret Keith, was first wife of the Rev. David Rose, Episcopal clergyman at Lethnot, and had four children, all of whom died early and unmarried.[1]

Of the two sons born to David Wysse of Mains of Thornton, David the elder settled on the lands of Drumnagair. He was killed by one of his own oxen. His tombstone in the parish churchyard of Laurencekirk, bears that he died November 1712, aged twenty-two years. Some verses on the event of his death are preserved in the family. Alexander, the second son, continued the male line of the House.

Some time after his marriage, David Wysse sold his estate of Mains of Thornton, and took up his residence at Mains of Laurieston, a small estate in the parish of St Cyrus, Kincardineshire. He purchased for his son Alexander the estate of Lunan, Forfarshire, on which that gentleman settled in his father's lifetime. At the death of his wife, Margaret Keith, David Wysse left Laurieston, and resided in Montrose, where he married Margaret Burnet of Monboddo, widow of Alexander Steele, Esq. Of this marriage there was no issue. He bequeathed considerable sums to the kirk sessions of Lunan, Montrose, St Cyrus, and Laurencekirk, for behoof of the poor in these respective parishes; and presented a set of silver communion cups to the kirk session of Lunan.

Alexander Wyse of Lunan was twice married. He married, first,

---

[1] By a second marriage, the Rev. David Rose had two children, a son and daughter. The son was the Honourable George Rose, grandfather of Lord Strathnairn.

April 1719, Jean, younger daughter of Peter Turnbull, Esq.[1] of Smithy Hill, a cadet of the old family of Turnbull of Strathcathro, by his wife, Euphan, daughter of William Henderson, Esq. of Hallyards.[2] Of this marriage was born a daughter, who married John Ritchie, merchant, Montrose; their son James married a daughter of the Right Reverend John Ochterlonie, Bishop of Brechin, and left a son, James Ritchie, of Bearhill, town-clerk of Brechin.

Alexander Wyse of Lunan espoused, secondly, in 1727, Margaret Strachan, daughter of George Strachan, Esq., burgess of Montrose, descended from the Monboddo branch of the House of Thornton, and father's sister of Sir John Strachan, Bart. of Thornton, who died in 1844. Of this marriage were born five sons and nine daughters.

Elizabeth, eldest daughter, baptized 3d February 1728, married, 16th June 1747, Alexander Wyse, merchant, Montrose.

Margaret, second daughter, baptized 21st April 1731, married, 15th November 1749, the Rev. Henry Ogilvie, minister of Lunan.[3] Of this marriage were born five sons and three daughters. John, the eldest son, married Miss Clegg, and resided at St Cyrus; the second son became a colonel in the British army, and Henry, the third son, was a lieutenant in the navy. Isabel, the youngest daughter, baptized 3d May 1766, married, 30th July 1790, the Rev. James Scott, minister of Benholme;

---

[1] David Edgar of Keithock was husband of the elder daughter of Peter Turnbull, Esq. of Smithy Hill. He subscribes as a contracting party the marriage settlement of Alexander Wyse of Lunan, dated 15th April 1719.

[2] William Henderson of Hallyards, parish of Meigle, Perthshire, claimed descent from Andrew Henderson, steward to the Earl of Gowrie, "the man in armour" of the Gowrie Conspiracy, to whom the King was mainly indebted for his escape.

[3] The Rev. Henry Ogilvie was celebrated for the fervour and unction of his pulpit prelections, and his other ministerial qualities. He was son of the Rev. Thomas Ogilvie, minister of Coupar-Angus, and his elder brother was Wedderburn Ogilvie, Esq. of Islabank, parish of Ruthven, Forfarshire.

she died 16th April 1838, leaving two sons, Dr Hercules Scott, Professor of Moral Philosophy in King's College, Aberdeen, and Dr John Scott, an eminent physician in London; also two daughters, Anne, who married the Rev. John Clegg, minister of Bervie, and another, who married the Rev. Dr Trail, Professor of Divinity in the University of Aberdeen. Mrs Margaret Ogilvie or Wise, died 12th July 1803 (Fasti Eccl. Scot.).

The remaining children of Alexander Wyse, and his second wife, Margaret Strachan, were as under:

David, baptized 29th March 1730.

Katherine, baptized 15th March 1733. Married John Wright, merchant, Montrose.

Isabel, baptized 27th January 1736. Married Colin Alison, merchant, Montrose, and had issue.

Anna, baptized 6th March 1737. Married J. Leslie, shipowner.

Alexander, baptized 18th July 1738. Died young.

Mary, baptized 13th January 1740. Married Peter Will, Dundee, and had two sons, Andrew, who entered the army, and, after many distinguished services during the Peninsular war and at Waterloo, died a captain in the 92d Regiment; and the Rev. James Will, successively minister of the parishes of Ruthven and Guthrie, in the county of Forfar; he died 3d May 1818, aged fifty-eight. An expert genealogist, Mr Will collected some of the materials used in the present narrative.

James, baptized 15th March 1741. Died young.

Jean, baptized 3d July 1742. Died in infancy.

Jean, baptized 20th August 1743.

Helen, baptized 19th February 1745. Married Captain Spink.

John, baptized 27th December 1747; died *s.p.*

Henry, baptized 8th October 1749. Died young (Parish Register of Lunan).

On the 26th December 1749, Alexander Wyse of Lunan executed a settlement of his affairs, nominating as his executors his son-in-law, the Rev. Henry Ogilvie, minister of Lunan, and his brother-in-law, Lieutenant James Strachan. He entrusted them with the administration of "eighteen thousand merks Scots money," which was to be applied to the support of his widow and for division among his children, "secluding David Wise, his eldest son." David subscribes the will as one of two witnesses; he writes his name David *Wise*, and thereafter this mode of spelling the family name universally obtained among the members of his House.

David Wise of Lunan was a person of remarkable mechanical skill. One of the first in Scotland to recognise the importance of employing machinery in the art of weaving, he invented a machine for cotton-spinning about the same time that Hargreaves of Lancashire produced his spinning-jenny in 1764. To make provision for the other members of his father's family, he disposed of the paternal inheritance.

David Wise married Grizel, daughter of Thomas Henderson, Esq. of Grange of Barry, by his wife Grizel,[1] daughter of John Scott, jun., merchant, Dundee, and his wife Grizel, daughter of John Brown, Esq. of Horn.[2] Mr Brown, who for ten years held office as a magistrate in Dundee, took an active part in defending the town against General Monk, who besieged it in October 1651. In defending the breach he fell mortally wounded, on the 6th October 1651 (Monuments, etc., in Scotland, vol. ii., p. 213).

John Scott, maternal grandfather of Mrs Grizel Henderson or Wise,

[1] The contract of marriage between Thomas Henderson of Grange of Barry and Grizel Scott is preserved among the Hillbank family papers. It is dated 24th April 1724, and is in the handwriting of the bride's cousin, John Wedderburn, son of Sir Alexander Wedderburn, Bart. of Blackness.

[2] Among the Hillbank papers is preserved the contract of marriage between John Scott and his wife, Grizel Brown, dated at Dundee, 5th May 1699; it is subscribed by Sir Alexander Wedderburn, Bart., of Blackness, town-clerk of Dundee, as one of the witnesses.

was eldest son of John Scott, Esq., Provost of Dundee, who with several sons, had eight daughters, who married into families of territorial rank. They united the Houses of Wedderburn, Henderson of Barry, Graham of Balmuir, Guthrie of Craigie, Guthrie of Taybank, and Hay, Bart. of Park.

David Wise and his wife Grizel Henderson had six sons and six daughters. The daughters were Johanna, Grace, Margaret, Elizabeth, Rachel, and Catherine. Johanna, the eldest daughter, married Josiah Maxton, merchant; Grace, the second daughter, married J. Thoms, Esq. of Clepington, Forfarshire, and Rumgallah and Pitscottie, Fifeshire, and had issue; Catherine, the youngest daughter, married C. Smith, and left issue. Of the sons, Alexander, William, and James, died young; and David and Peter died unmarried. David Wise of Lunan died in September 1803.

Thomas, the eldest son, became a physician, and proceeding to Jamaica, there acquired the valuable estate of Claremont, in the parish of Hanover. Returning to his native country, he purchased the estate of Hillbank, in the county of Forfar. He married Anne, second daughter of William Chalmers, Esq. of Glenericht, Perthshire, by his wife, Anna, daughter of James Hay, Esq. of Seggieden.

The family of Chalmers of Glenericht are entitled to more than a passing notice. Descended from the ancient House of Chalmers of that ilk, and less remotely representing the House of Chalmers of Lawers, they possessed relatives in Fifeshire, from whom sprung the celebrated theologian and orator Dr Thomas Chalmers. Settling in Dundee, where he became an opulent merchant, William Chalmers married Euphan, daughter of Andrew Wardroper, merchant, the representative of an old family of prosperous burgesses of Dundee, now extinct in the male line. Andrew Wardroper was provost of the burgh; his father, Thomas

Wardroper, a prosperous merchant, also held office in the magistracy, as did Andrew Wardroper, his paternal grandfather.

Of the marriage of William Chalmers and Euphan Wardroper were born two sons. Andrew, the younger, entered the Royal Navy, and became a lieutenant; after much active and distinguished service, he died at Plymouth, having been injured by the fall of a block of timber on board his vessel. William, the elder son, became town-clerk of Dundee, and purchased the estate of Glenericht, in the county of Perth. He married, first, Anna, daughter of James Hay, Esq. of Seggieden, and by this union became father of two daughters, Euphemia, who married William Pitcairn, merchant, Dundee, and Anne, who, as before stated, married Thomas Wise of Hillbank. William Chalmers of Glenericht married, secondly, Margaret, sister of General Sir Kenneth Mackenzie Douglas, Bart. of Glenbervie. Of this marriage were born one son and two daughters. Jessy, elder daughter, married William Macpherson, Esq. of Blairgowrie; Margaret, the younger daughter, married the Rev. Allan Macpherson, younger brother of the proprietor of Blairgowrie, and chaplain in the service of the Hon. East India Company.

William, son of William Chalmers of Glenericht and Margaret Mackenzie, was born in Dundee in 1785. After a distinguished career as a student at the University of St Andrews, he entered the army in his eighteenth year. During the Peninsular war he greatly distinguished himself, being present in twelve general engagements. In command of Hanoverian troops, at the battle of the Pyrenees, he was severely wounded; and in acknowledgment of his valour he received the Grand Cross of the Hanoverian Order. At the battle of Waterloo he had three horses shot under him. Retiring from active service in 1816, he established his residence at Dundee. He became Lieutenant-General, was Colonel of the 78th Regiment, and was successively nominated C.B. and K.C.H. From

Her Majesty the Queen he received the honour of knighthood. Sir William Chalmers died 2d June 1860.[1]

[1] A family tombstone in the Howff, Dundee, belonging to the family of Chalmers of Glenericht, is thus inscribed :

Heir Resteth in the Lord ANDREW
WARDROPER Merchant In Dundee Who
Depairted This Lyfe The 23 Day of Jaunuary 1698
years And of His Age 72 years
As also Here Lyes THOMAS WARDROPER Merch^t and
sometime Bailie of Dundee who Died the 21st Day
of September 1724 and of his age 63 years

En Memory of
ANDREW WARDROPER who died 6th May 1770
and his Wife MARGARET SCOTT

also in Memory of
WILLIAM CHALMERS Merchant in Dundee
and his Wife EUPHAN WARDROPER
daughter of ANDREW WARDROPER

and their son
WILLIAM CHALMERS of Glenericht
Town-Clerk of Dundee
who died 2nd August 1817 aged 75 years

and his Wife MARGARET MACKENZIE
Daughter of KENNETH MACKENZIE Esquire
who died 16th November 1800

and also of their son
Lieutenant-General Sir WILLIAM CHALMERS C.B. K.C.H.
who died 2d June 1860 aged 75 years

and his Wife ANNE PAGE
who died 22d March 1851 aged 45 years

and of their children
WILLIAM their eldest son who died at sea
on the 14th March 1848 aged 21 years
ANNE JANE who died 5th October 1850 aged 16 years
JESSIE MACPHERSON who died 7th February 1837
aged 22 months
EMILY ISABELLA DISNEY, who died 10th March 1846
aged 9 years.

William Chalmers of Glenericht, father of Sir William, married, thirdly, Barbara Brown, whose brother, Laurence Brown, married the niece of George Constable of Wallace Craigie—the prototype in the "Antiquary" of *Jonathan Oldbuck*; their son, Lieut.-Colonel Brown Constable, now inherits the estate.

Of the marriage of Thomas Wise of Hillbank,[1] and his wife, Anne Chalmers, were born four sons and two daughters. Anne, the elder daughter, is unmarried. Barbara, the younger daughter, married John Thoms, Esq. of Pitscottie, Fifeshire, and has issue.

David, the eldest son, died young. William, the second son, entered the military service of the Hon. East India Company, and became a captain. On the death of his father in 1816, he succeeded to the estate of Hillbank. He died unmarried 4th November 1845. Patrick Josiah, fourth son, was a merchant in India. For many years he administered the public affairs of the independent kingdom of Tipperah, Easter Bengal, to the entire satisfaction of the sovereign, and the best interests of the people. He possesses large estates in Ireland, and resides at Rostellan Castle, county Cork.

Thomas Alexander Wise, M.D., third son of Thomas Wise and Anne Chalmers, succeeded to the estate of Hillbank on the death of William, his elder brother, in 1845. For many years a physician in the service of the Hon. East India Company, he held staff appointments at various important stations. He was some time Secretary to the Committee of Instruction, Bengal, and Principal of the Hooghly and Dacca Colleges. He is author of various professional and educational works.

[1] Thomas Wise of Claremont and Hillbank acquired a portion of ground in the Howff, or ancient burial-place at Dundee, which he enclosed with an iron railing, as a place of sepulture for the members of his House. A large pavement stone within the enclosure is adorned with the family shield, and inscribed thus : "Thomas Wise, Armiger de Hillbank, sibi et suis proprium sepulcrum designandi causa hunc lapidem posuit."

Dr Wise married, first, Emily Isabella, daughter of J. Fownes Norton Disney, Esq., of Dublin, and niece of Lieutenant-General Disney, a distinguished soldier. Through her mother, Anne, daughter of Thomas Prendergast, Esq., barrister-at-law, she was niece of Sir Jeffrey Prendergast, K.C.B. She died 12th May 1839, leaving four sons and two daughters.

Thomas Allan Macpherson, merchant, Dacca, died 1859, *s.p.*

William Henry, 64th Bengal N.I., died 1858.

Emilius Somerset, died young.

James Fownes Norton, M.D., on the Staff of the Indian Government.

Anna Margaret, married Colonel Nicolson of the 64th Regiment.

Henrietta Babington, married Clement F. Lawless, Esq. of Kilcrone, county Cork.

Dr Wise married, secondly, Harriet Elizabeth, daughter of William Phelan, Esq. of Rock Abbey, county Tipperary, representative of an old Milesian House. Of this marriage were born:

Frederic Donelly, died 1868, *s.p.*

Alexander Josiah Patrick, married 9th August 1870, Julia, second daughter of J. A. Woods, Esq. of Benton Hall, Northumberland.

Henry Douglas.

William Bernard.

Allan Hay.

APPENDIX.

No. I.

EXTRACTS FROM A MANUSCRIPT ENTITLED, "A GENEALOGIE OF THE BARONS OF THE MEARNES UNTO THE YEAR OF GOD 1578," IN THE POSSESSION OF MRS BARCLAY ALLARDICE.

Alexander Strachan, Laird of Thorntoun, divided the lands of Thorntoun to his two sones, viz., Alex^r and John; Alex^r he got the lands of Thorntoun, and to John he gave the lands of Monboddo. Alex^r married Elizabeth, dau^r to the Lord Hay, and had succession an son named John, who succeeded to the lands of Thorntoun, and married Janet Ross, dau^r to the Laird of Auchloson in Marr, and begot on her an son called David Strachan, who married Margaret Hay, dau^r to the Laird of Dalgatie, and had no succession ; this David Strachan deceased, after whose decease John Strachan of Dillivaird succeeded, who married Eliz. Straton, daughter to the Laird of Lauriestoun, and begate on her an son named Alex^r Alex^r, who married Katherine Erskine, daughter to the Laird of Dun, and begate on her a son named John, who married Margaret Livingston, dau^r to the Laird of Dunepace, and she had to him an son named Alexander, who married Eliz. Keith, dau^r to William, Earl Marischall.

(*Extinct.*)

MONBODDO STRACHAN.—Strachan, Laird of Monboddo, married Craigie's daughter Straton, and she had to him an son called Andrew Strachan, who married Ogill's daughter ffentoun, and she had to him James, who married Burrowfield's daughter Garden, and she had to him an son named John, who married Eupham Strachan, daughter to John Strachan of Dillivaird, and she had to him James Strachan, who married Marjory Ramsay, daughter to uncq'le William Ramsay of Balmain.

No. II.

MEMORIAL OF THE ANTIENT FAMILY OF STRACHANS, MORE PARTICULARLY OF THE HOUSE OF THORNTON.[1]

This sirname is local—as others of the greatest antiquity—and has been according to antient custom taken from lands—the barony of Strachan, in the county of Kin-

[1] Macfarlane's Genealogical Collections, MS. [*circa* 1735], Advocates Library, Edinburgh, vol. ii., p. 101.

carden, when sirnames began first to be taken up with us, which, as an agreed point, was not before the reign of King David the 1st, who came to the throne anno 1124.

The first using the sirname of Strachan that has occurred to me was Valdevus de Strachan or Stratheychan, as it's called in the most antient charters and deeds, who, with consent, cum consensu Radulphi de Strachathen heredis sui gave Deo & canonicis Sancti Andre terres de Black Larkh, to which deed Malcolunus Archideaconus Sancti Andræ is a witness,[1] and appears to be toward the end of the reign of King Malcolm the 4th, circiter annum 1160.

Johannis de Strachetheyn, his son, flourished in the reign of King Alexander the 2d. In the voucher here cited,[2] he is designed filius et heres Radulphi de Strachethyn, when he makes over to the Abbot and Convent of Dunfermling the lands of Belheldys pro salute suæ, &c. This deed of mortification is confirmed by King Alexander 3d, the 2d October, the 30th year of the king's reign, that is, in the year of our Lord, 1273.[3] To this deed there are witnesses : Wilhelmus de Sancti Claro, tunc vicecomes de Edinburgh ; Wilhelmus Fraser, Cancellarus Scotiæ ; & Johannis de Lindsay, tunc Camerarius Scotiæ. By the heir general and at law the barony of Strachan came by marriage to Sir Alexander Fraser, who was Lord High Chamberlain to King Robert the Bruce, as the original charter granted by that prince yet extant testifies : Robertus Die gratia sciatis nos dedisse dilecto, & fideli nostro Alexandro Fraser militi omnes and singulas terras de Strachethyne de Essely et Auchinerooks faciendo nobis et heredibus nostris dictus Alexander, et heredes sui forensicum servitium quantum pertinet ad prædictam barouium. Datum apud Air primo die Novembris anno regni nostri decimo,[4] that is, in the year 1316. By the grandchild and heir of this Sir Alexander, by Sir John Fraser his eldest son, Dame Margaret Fraser, the barony of Strachan, Fetteresso, Dalpersy, &c., came by marriage to Sir William Keith of that ilk, Marishall of Scotland in the reign of King David 3d. For there is a charter still extant,[5] granted by Willielmus de Keith, Mariscallus Scotiæ et Domina Margareta Fraser, sponsa sua de terris baroniæ de Strachethyne in vicecomitatu de Kincardine tenendis, &c., de Roberto de Keith nepoti nostro, to which the granters append their seals,[6] anno 1375.

But altho' the barony of Strachan or Strachethyn, which is one and the same, went out of the male line of the antient proprietors by an heir generall to the family of Keith, yet the antient house of the Strachans still subsists in the male line by a younger branch, who were possessed of the lands of Monicabo, &c., in the county of Kincarden, for in the reign of King David 2d, Sir James Strachan, Jacobus de Stratheyhen, miles, as he is designed[7] in a charter, Alexandro Fraser, militi, who obtained the lands and barony of Thornton, in the Mearns or shyre of Kincairden, by the marriage of Agneta de Thornton, as the charter granted by King David Bruce bears,

[1] Chartulary of the Priory of St Andrews, MSS., in the library of the most noble family of Panmure, vide page 120.
[2] Chartulary of Dumfermling in the Lawyers' Library at Edinburgh, manuscript.
[3] Ibidem.
[4] Original Charter I have seen and perused in the custody of Sir Peter Fraser of Dores, Baronet.
[5] Ibidem.
[6] The sealls to the charter are intire in the charter-chest of the House of Dores.
[7] Charter I have seen in the hands of the Lord Salton, and confirmed by an antient manuscript of the family of Thornton transmitted to me in 1705 by a very aged gentleman, one Mr Strachan.

the 34th year of his reign, dated apud Forfar. This Sir James Strachan, the first of this antient and honourable race who had the barony of Thornton, had two sons, Duncan the eldest, who had the lands of Monucubo, &c., in the county of Kincairden, and a part of the lands of Keir, in the shyre of Perth, who left only one daughter, Cristiana Strachan, who was married to Sir Malcom Fleeming of Biggar,[1] ancestor to the present Earl of Wigton, with whom he got the estate of Monucubo, &c., which continued long in that family. The second son, Sir James Strachan, the first of the House of Thornton, was Sir John Strahan, to whom his father gave the estate and lands of Thornton, and obtained the honour of Knighthood from King Robert the 2d. For he, Johannes de Strachethyn, miles, is witnes to a charter by Willielmus de Keith, Mariscallus Scotiæ et Margareta Fraser, sponsa sua Roberto de Keith eorum filio de omnibus et singulis terris nostris de Strathethyne cum omnibus forrestis ejusdem &c. forresta de Culpenach et Corlothery. Datum apud Kincairden 10 Decembris anno 1375; which charter is ratified and confirmed by King Robert 2d the 27 of December 1376.[2]

Alexander Strachan of Thornton was the next in the lineal succession in this very antient family, and flourished in the reign of King Robert 3d; and afterward he is witnes to a charter still extant, in the custody of the Earl of Wigton, granted by Robert, Duke of Albany, Earl of Fife and Monteith, Malcolmo Fleeming de Biggar, militi, delecto fllio nostro de terris de Torwood, dated 8 June 1414.[3] He married Margaret Hay, daughter to John Hay of Tillibothy[4] and Enzie, and had by her Alexander Strachan, designed in the lifetime of his father, as I take it, Monboddo; under this title and designation he is one of the Gentlemen of the Inquest, whereby Sir Alexander Fraser of Philorth is served heir to Sir Alexander Fraser, his grandfather, before Patrick Barclay, Sherriff of Kincairden, decimo quarto die mensis Aprilis 1461.[5] This Alex^r Strachan, afterwards designed of Thornton, married Margaret Ross, daughter of   Ross of Kilravock,[6] and had John Strachan, his son and heir, who had a charter of his estate under the Great Seall of King James the 3d.[7] He married Margaret, daughter of   Straiton of Lauriston, an antient family in the county of Kincairden, and had by her, David his heir, and John the second son, who carried on the line of succession of the House of Thornton. This gentleman resigned the fee of his estate in [the hands of] the Crown, in favours of David Strachan, his son and heir-apparent, reserving his own liferent, upon which he had an investiture under the Great Seal in the year 1487,[8] and to Marion Hay, his wife, and their heirs. This David Strachan, Feodilarius de Thornton, as I find him designed, executed the office of Justice-Clerk in the beginning of the reign of King James the 4th, anno 1492,[9] and he discharged the office till the 1497, it was conferred on Mr Richard Lawson of the Harrys. This David Strachan of Thornton, when he came to be at the head of the family, having no issue-male, and it seems but little prospect of any, resigns the fee of the estate of

[1] Iipdem MSS.
[2] Charter I have seen in the hands of Sir Peter Fraser of Darus, Baronet.
[3] Carta penes Comitem de Wigton I have seen in his charter-chest.
[4] Mr Strachan's Manu-cript History of the House of Thornton.
[5] This Inquest I have seen in the hands of the Lord Salton.
[6] Mr Strachan's MSS.
[7] Said archives.
[8] Charter in the Register of the Great Seal in the publick archives at Edinburgh.
[9] Chartulary of Arbroth in the Lawyers' Library at Edbr ad annum 1492, and the archives of the Officers of State, MSS., vol. 2d.

Appendix.

Thornton, in favours of Mr Alexander Strachan, his nephew by his brother, reserving his own liferent, and a liferent to Marion Hay, his spouse, and also a liferent of John Strachan, his brother, and a liferent to his brother's wife, Margaret Durham, all which is ratified and approven by a charter under the Great Seal in 1421, August 1.[1] This David Strachan of Thornton was married to Marion Hay, daughter to William, Earl of Errol,[2] but, dying without issue, was succeeded by his brother and heir.

John Strachan of Thornton, who acquired the ward of the lands of Midleton, in the county of Kincairden, which is confirmed by a charter under the Great Seal in our publick archives, anno 1585. He married Marg^t Durham, daughter of Durham of Grange, a right antient family in the shire of Forfar, and had Alexander Strachan of Thornton, his son and heir, who married Margaret Hay, daughter of Hay of Dalgelly in Aberdeenshire,[3] and again, Isobell, daughter of David Falconer of Halkerton,[4] and had issue John Strachan of Thornton, his heir, and severall daughters, which brought a great alliance to the family; one was married to Wood of Ballegno; Marg^t to William Ramsay of Balmain, in the Mearns, and afterward to Ugston of that ilk; Jean to Henry Graham of Morphy, in the county of Kincairden; and all had issue.

John Strachan of Thornton is one of the great barons who sat and voted in the Parliament 1560, in the great turn of the Reformation, and that virtute tenure, a privilege the barons were never by any statute deprived of, altho' they had long disused their giving suit & presence in Parliament. But upon that occasion they came and gave their suffrages mostly for the Reformed doctrine.[5] He married Margaret Erskine, daughter to John Erskine of Dun by Dame Margaret Ruthven, Countes Dowager of Buchan, daughter to William, Lord Ruthven, ancestor to the Earl of Gowrie,[6] by whom he had John Strachan of Thornton, his heir and successor, and Alexander Strachan of Goosesley, whose heir of line and at law was married to John Midleton of Cadham, mother by her to Livt-Generall John Midleton, raised to the honour of Earl of Midleton by King Charles the 2d, in the year 166 . There was a third and younger son, of whom my author, a worthy gentleman of this family, Mr Strachan, says, came and issued the Strachans of Phesdo, &c.

John Strachan of Thornton was by the Privy Council named one of the Commissioners for the shire of Kincairden, that were to keep the peace within the bounds of their county, and for discovering and detecting seminary preists and Jesuites in the 1590.[7] This gentleman married Isobell Livingston, of Mr Alexander Livingston of Dunnipace, in the county of Stirling,[8] who was Director of the Chancery in the reign of Queen Mary,[9] by Jean his wife, daughter of Robert, the 2d Lord Elphingston.[10] By this lady the Laird of Thornton had a most numerous issue, no fewer than eight sons and severall daughters, vizt:

[1] Charter in the Registers of the Great S all in the publick archives.
[2] Mr Strachan's accot of the Family of Thornton. I find him a great confident of the House of Erroll from the 1483 and downward.
[3] Ibidem. [4] Ibidem. [5] List of the Parliament in Mr Keith's Collection.
[6] Birth brieff of the Midletons. I have seen ch Joanni Strathachin de Thornton et Margarete Liston, sue sponse, &c., de terris de Bridgeton in bar. de Thornton infra Vic. de Kincardin, 29 Janij 1553, ch. 176, lib. 21. She seems to be only a second wife. But 'tis possible that by the error of the transcriber it may be Liston instead of Erskine.
[7] Mr David Calderwood's Church History.
[8] Midleton's birth brieff I have seen in Mr Anderson's hands.
[9] Carta in publicis archives, ad annum 1558, &c. [10] Ibidem.

Appendix.

Alexander, the heir of the family.
William, the second son.
David.
Arthur.
John, of whom the gentlemen at London are descended, as I am informed.
Thomas.
James.
Archibald.

Katherine, the eldest daughter of John Strachan of Thornton and Isobell Livingston, was married to David Forbes of Corss, mother by him to Patrick Forbes of Corss, who was Bishop of Aberdeen in the reign of King Charles the first, and dyed in the 1635, a little before the breaking out of the troubles. Her second son was Sir Arthur Forbes of Castle Forbes, in Ireland, whose son was Earl of Granard in that realm. Her third son by Corss was Sir William Forbes of Craigievar.[1]

Elizabeth, the second daughter of Thornton, was married to John Midleton of that ilk, in the county of Forfar, ancestor to the Earl of Midleton;[2] of her that family lineally sprang.

Margaret, another daughter, was married to　　　　Symer of Belyordie,[3] repute an antient family in Forfar shyre.

Mary, another daughter, was married to William Rait of Halgreen, a very antient family as any in all the county of Forfar, and had a daughter Elizabeth, who was married to Sir George Auchinleck of Balmano, in Perth shyre, who was one of the Senators of the Colledge of Justice in the reign of King James the 6th, of whom is come a most numerous and far spread progeny and descendants. To this John Strachan of Thornton succeeded Alexander, his eldest son and heir, who married Dame Sarah Douglas, daughter to Sir William Douglas of Glenbervy,[4] who succeeded to the estate and dignity of Earl of Angus in the 1588; and had by her a son, his heir, viz., Sir Alexander Strachan of Thornton, who was by the special favour of his Majesty King Charles the first, raised to the degree and dignity of a knight-baronet, soon after the first institution of that honourary order in the year 1625, which was just upon his accession to the crown; I have not seen the precise date of the patent, but in a Minute-Book of that time, I have seen it marked to be of the date of 28 May 1625.[5] It is, as all other patents of baronetts at that time and long afterwards were, to the heirs-male at large of the first patentee, and it must have been uniform with the others granted by the king at that time, which are constantly to the heredibus masculis of him who first received the honour. But tho' this patent had passed the sealls in due form as the law directs in the lik cases, and other two gentlemen beside Sir Alexander Strachan of Thornton, viz., Sir William Douglas of Glenbervy, who was the Earl of Angus's son, and Sir David Livingston of Dunnipace, had also their patents of a prior date, the 14th July 1625, yet the king, as the fountain of honour, and by virtue of his royal prerogative, and because his Majesty, as he declares himself, that he had promised another gentleman, Sir Donald McDonald of Slate, the precedency of all the other three baronetts, who had been created before him. The charge is odd and singular,

[1] Mr Strachan's MSS., compared with other vouchers all agreeing in this.
[2] Midleton's birth brieff.　　[3] Mr Strachan's Manuscript.
[4] History of the House of Angus continued.
[5] This Minute-Book belonged to Mr David Sibbald, who was depute-keeper of the Great Seal under Chancellour Hay, and from his son, Sir Robert Sibbald, that great antiquary, I had the use of it, and is here my voucher.

it establishes fully the baronettship of the House of Thornton, and showes that Sir Alexander Strachan, Sir William Douglas, and Sir David Livingston, were all three baronetts before the 24 July 1625. It bears, the soveraign the king declaring Quod dictus Dominus Donaldus Mcdonald de Slate heredes sui masculi et assignati locum habebunt ante Dominum Willielmum Douglas de Glenbervie Militem Baronettum, Dominum Alexandrum Strachan de Thornton Militem Baronettum et Dominum David Livingston de Dunnipace Militem Baronettum non obstante quod Ipsorum litteræ Patentes sub sigillo nostro hactenus Expedite sunt hac Ratione quod prins quam nos Ipsorum Signaturus Signavimus Expresse nobis pacti sunt et Concederunt quod dictus Dominus Donaldus Mcdonald ante ipsos haberet locum ut permittitur.

This is a demonstrative proof that the patent of Sir Alexander Strachan of Thornton, raising him to the baronettship, was the next immediately following Sir William Douglas of Glenbervy, which from the patent itself is of the date the 28 May 1625, and the very same day that Thornton's passed the sealls. But the king's Majesty having signed Sir William Douglas's warrant first, gave him the precedency of the other, so that the matter being thus settled, I know none has the precedency of the heir-male of the House of Thornton, but Sir William Gordon of Gordonston, and Sir Robert Douglas of Glenbervy; in that case Thornton's heir-male, John Strachan of Thornton, who now claims it, is the third barrouett in the list or order and rank of the precedency of the knights-baronetts.

This Sir Alexander Strachan of Thornton, the first baronet of the family, was succeeded by a second Sir Alexander, his only son, who matched with   of the Lindsays, of the noble family of Balcarras; but he had no issue, neither had he any with the Countes-Dowager of Marshall, Dame Margaret, daughter of James, Lord Ogilvy, with whom he lived long in France, where he died during the exile of King Charles the Second. Upon his death, the baronettship went by the patent, that limited the honour to his heirs-male, to Sir James Strachan, who was a clergyman minister, I think, at Keith, beyond Aberdeen. He married Margaret Forbes, of the family of Watterton, and had a son, Sir James Strachan of Thornton, who may be perhaps the father of Francis Strachan, the Jesuite at Paris, who has now the matter, tho' perhaps not with all the formalitys requisite, resign'd the title of the baronetship of the family of Thornton, to another gentleman, John Strachan, who resides in Sweden, and designs himself by the title of Thornton, as the heir-male of the family, and in one of his letters he acknowledges that his own grandfather and this gentleman's grandfather were two brothers. I take them for certain to be both descended of two of the younger sons, the second and third son of John Strachan of Thornton, and his wife Isobell Livingston, daughter of Mr Alexander Livingston of Dunnipace, so if this gentleman wants a genealogical birth brieff of his grandfather, it could be made out from undoubted authoritys and vouchers, very authentically.

The cadets of the House of Thornton were the Strachans of Carmylie, in Angus, near Arbroath, are now a creditable family of the name of Strachan, and allied twice or thrice with the daughters of the family of Panmure, as may be seen from the account of the House of Panmure, in the peerage of Scotland, and it's observable that the Strachans of Carmylie matched also with the Lord Gray's family.

The Strachans of Glenkindy have always been reputed the first and eldest cadet of the family of Thornton, for in the reign of King David the 2d, the first of them obtained the lands of Glenkindy, &c., &c., by the marriage of Mariota de

Garrioch, a lady whom the Earl of Marr calls his cousine, in the grant of the lands to them and their heirs, which charter, the originall, I have seen and perused.

The Strachans of Scotston were descended of a younger brother of the House of Thornton; in the reign of King James the 4th, Alexander Strachan of Scotston acquires from Sir William Edmondston of Duntreath, in the west in Stirling shyre, the lands and estate of Colloden, in Invernes shyre, which is ratified by a charter under the Great Seall in the year 1506, which I have seen in the Registers of the Privy Seall, in the publick archives at Edinburgh, in the year 1506.

Of the family of Thornton was descended, as I have been credibly informed, Mr David Strachan, who was minister and parson of Fettercairn, in the Mearns, and upon the recommendation of the Earl of Midleton (who was the Prime Minister of State upon the Restoration of King Charles the 2d) was promotted to the Episcopall see of Brechin, anno 1661, where he sat for the space of nine years, even till his death in the 1671.[1]

I am assured from many hands that the gentlemen at London, the councillour at law, Dr Strachan, and his brothers, are descended of the House of Thornton; their great-grandfather was John Strachan, a younger son of the family of Thornton; that he had a small estate called Dyhill, near Banff; that his son was a clergyman, a minister at Aberdeen; that his son again was bred to the Church, was a minister, and Professor of Divinity in the University of Edinburgh, before the Revolution in 1689. The gentlemen at London, I say, are his sons.

To conclude—There is a mortification by John Strachan of Thornton, with consent of David Strachan, his son and heir-apparent, of eleven merks of annuity to a chaplainry in the paroch church of Aberluthnot, in the year 1490,[2] which is fitt to be noticed, since here is collected all that has occurred to me in a course of many years, relating to the Strachans, more particularly the House of Thornton, that have a baronetship in their family.

[The following note is added in the handwriting of Macfarlane.]

Charta Waldevi de Strathechan cum consensu Ranulfi heredis sui concessa canonicis Beati Andreæ Apostoli in Scotia de terra de Blackeroch extra silvam, cum communi pastura inter Feyhan[3] et De,[3] ad sexaginta Porcos, et ad sexaginta vaccas cum fitibus suis donec trium fuerint annorum, et ad viginti equos cum sequela sua donec quatuor fuerint annorum, &c. Testibus Magistro Lawrencio Archidiacono Sancti Andreæ Dᵒ Malcolmo Archidiacono Abirdonensi. Ranulfo filio Walderi, &c.—Registᵐ Prioratus Sancti Andreæ, p. 337.

[1] Memoirs of the Bishops of Brechin, MSS.
[2] Collection of Mortifications by Sir John Scott from the Registers.
[3] Nunc, ut puto, Feuch et Dy, rivuli in Baronia de Strathachan, nunc Strachan, in vicecomitatu de Kincardin.

INDEX.

Aan, river, 1.
Aberluthnot, chapel of, 27.
Aberdeen, Gilbert, Bishop of, 3, 11.
   Malcolm, Archdeacon of, 112.
   Strachans in, 3, 18, 19.
   William, Bishop of, 27, 31.
Aberdein, Francis, of Keithock, 96.
Achenerooks, lands of, 2, 107.
Adam, John, 35.
Affleck, Sir George, of Balmanno, 44.
Aikenhead, David, 55.
Alexander II., 2, 107.
   III., 107.
Alison, Colin, 99.
Allardice, Mrs Barclay, 106.
   Thomas, 47, 48, 64.
Ancrum, battle of, 4.
Arbirney, lands of, 53.
Arbroath, Malcolm, Abbot of, 17.
   William, Abbot of, 10.
Arbuthnot, Andrew, of Pitcarles, 29, 55.
   Christian, 75.
   David, 14.
   Elizabeth, 24.
   Principal Alexander, 29.
   Robert, of that ilk, 29, 38.
Arnbarrow, Alexander Strachan-in, 35.
   lands of, 41, 56.
Auchenbrake, lands of, 34.
Auchinlar, or Achlair, lands of, 7, 9, 10, 11, 15.
Auchinleck, Elizabeth, 52.
   Hew, of that ilk, 14.
   Janet, 5.
   John, 14.
   Sir George, of Balmanno, 36, 110.
   Sir John, of Pitrichie, 52.
   Thomas, 73.

Auchloson, Ross of, 106.
Auchterlony—*see* Ochterlony.

Bagnano, Duke di, 95.
Balbegno, woods of, 108.
Balcherge, lands of, 5.
Balhousie, lands of, 17.
   Strachaus of, 17, 18.
Balmaddie, Strachans in, 23.
Balmain, lands of, 2, 29.
Balmakewan, lands of, 56, 60, 64.
Balmerino, Lord, 40.
Balmuir, Grahams of, 101.
Barclay, Anna, 86.
   Captain David, of Mathers, 86.
   Colonel David, of Urie, 86.
   Patrick, Sheriff of Mearns, 108.
Baronetcy, patent of, 91, 92, 111.
Beaton, Cardinal David, 27, 28, 53.
Beattie, Catherine, 96.
   Dr James, 96.
   Robert, 20.
Bell, Sir David, 13, 14.
Belyordie, Symers of, 110.
Bent, lands of, 46, 65.
Beth, lands of, 1, 13.
Beton, John, of Auchinvoche, 15.
   Margaret, 15.
Birth-brieve of Sir John Orchardton of that ilk, 51, 52.
Blackerock, lands of, 1, 107, 112.
Blackhall, lands of, 5.
   William, of that ilk, 5.
Blair, William, of Bagillo, 42.
Boghall, lands of, 30.
"Book of Caerlaverock, the," 71.
Braidislies, lands of, 33, 65.

Branderawe, battle of, 95.
Bremner, Jane, of Attenbury, 71.
Brigtoun, lands of, 11, 27, 31, 45, 46, 48, 65, 109.
  Strachans in, 16, 23, 24.
Broadlands, lands of, 50.
Brown, Alicia, 17.
  Barbara, 104.
  Grizel, 100.
  John, of Horn, 100.
  Laurence, 104.
Buchan, Alexander, of Auchmacoy, 59, 60.
Burarton, Strachans of, 81.
Burnet, Margaret, of Monboddo, 97.
  Rev. Thomas, 55.
Burnett, Robert, of Elvick, 50.
  Sir Thomas, of Leys, 77.

CAIRNTOW, Strachans of, 15.
Caldhame, lands of, 33, 42, 53, 64, 68.
Cambystoun, lands of, 19.
Camera, Angus de, 11.
Carcary, lands of, 23, 25.
Cardenbarclay, lands of, 25.
Carmyllie, lands of, 7, 10-12.
  Strachans of, 7-17.
Carnegie, Captain Rennie Strachan, 91.
  Elizabeth, 90.
  Helen, 18.
  John, 91.
  John, of Kinnaird, 17, 23.
  Robert, 23, 29.
  Sir David, of Pitarrow, 90.
  Sir David, of Southesk, 90.
  Walter de, 25.
Cave, John, of Brentry, 84.
Chalmers, Andrew, 102.
  Anne, 101-104.
  Dr Thomas, 101.
  Emily, 103.
  Euphemia, 102.
  Jessy, 102, 103.
  Margaret, 102.
  Sir William, of Glenericht, 102, 103.
  the family of, of Glenericht, 101-104.
  William, of Glenericht, 101-104.
Chapelton, lands of, 19.
Charles I., 21, 40, 110.
  II., 21, 64, 109, 111, 112.
Charter of Adjudication, 68.
Charters of Charles I., 45, 46.
  Charles II., 65-67.

Charters—continued.
  David II., 107.
  Oliver Cromwell, 48.
  Robert II., 10, 11.
  Robert III., 11.
  Robert the Bruce, 107.
  Sir Thomas Maule of Panmure, 12, 13, 17.
  the family of Duff, 5.
  the family of Leslie, 2, 28, 29.
  Walter de Maule of Panmure, 8.
  Waltheof de Strachan, 107.
  William de Maule, 8, 9, 107, 108.
Christeson, Sir John, 31.
Christie, Thomas, 77, 80.
Claypotts, Strachans of, 7, 15, 16, 18, 20.
Cliffden, Strachans of, 82-84.
Colpnay, lands of, 50, 108.
Commission, Royal, to inquire into Cardinal Beaton's death, 28, 29.
Constable, George, 104.
  Lady Winifred, 72.
  Lieut.-Colonel Brown, 104.
  William M., 71.
Contract of alienation, 56, 57.
Conveth, lands of, 53.
Coolistown, lands of, 17.
Cowlie, lands of, 33.
Craighall, lands of, 53.
Craigie, Guthrie of, 101.
Craigichill, lands of, 53.
Craigneston, lands of, 38, 40.
Craufurd, John de, 11.
Crombie, Alexander, of Phesdo, 69.
Cromwell, Oliver, 21, 22.
Culloden, lands of, 6.
  Strachans of, 6, 26, 112.
Culquhorsy, lands of, 31.
Cunninghame, William, Earl of Glencairn, 30.

DANIEL, Colonel William, 58.
David I., 107.
  II., 6, 7, 25, 107, 111.
Dillevard, Strachans of, 106.
Dillon, Louisa, Lady Strachan, 94, 95.
Dilto, Moss of, 13.
Disney, Emily, 105.
  J. Fownes Norton, 105.
  Lieut.-General, 105.
Disposition of lands of Auchinlar, 9-11.
Dixon, Dr James, 87.

Index. 115

Donaldson, Catherine, 81, 82.
Douglas, Archibald, Earl of, 3.
   Archibald, Earl of Angus, 30.
   Elizabeth, 45.
   Marion, Lady Drum, 41.
   Sara, 33, 110.
   Sir James, of Dalkeith, 3.
   Sir Robert, of Glenbervie, 111.
   Sir William, of Glenbervie, 36, 45, 110, 111.
   William, Earl of Angus, 40.
   William of, 11.
Drummadicht, lands of, 7, 10, 11.
Drummond, Janet, 12, 13.
   Rev. Andrew, 13.
Drumnagair, lands of, 97.
Duliewards, lands of, 27.
Dunbar, Ninian, of Grangehill, 61.
Dunkeld, John, Bishop of, 11.
Durham, Margaret, 26, 27, 109.
   Sir William, of Grange, 26.
Dyhill, Strachans of, 112.

Echt, lands of, 31.
Edgar, David, of Keithock, 98.
Edmeston, lands of, 74.
Edmonston, Sir William, of Duntreath, 112.
Elphinstone, Alexander, 49.
   Jean, 109.
   Robert, 109.
Elton, Isaac, of White Staunton, 84.
   Mary Anne, 84.
Erigstoun, lands of, 61.
Erskine, Catherine, of Dun, 106.
   John, of Dun, 109.
   Margaret, 15, 109.
   Sir Robert, 11.
   Sir Thomas de, 3.
Essuly, or Esly, lands of, 2, 107.

Falconer, Alexander, of Halkerton, 46, 75.
   David, of Halkerton, 109.
   Isabel, of Halkerton, 29, 109.
Fettercairn, lands of, 34, 53, 107.
   Strachans of, 41, 48, 50, 56, 59, 75.
Flemyng, Sir David, of Biggar, 11.
   Sir Malcolm, of Biggar, 25, 108.
Fleschour, Andrew, 13.
Forbes, Barbara, 64-67.
   David, of Corse, 110.
   Elizabeth, 62, 64, 67; epitaph, 62, 63.

Forbes—*continued*.
   James, of Saach, 67.
   James, of Thornton, 67.
   John, of Echt, 33.
   Margaret, 111.
   Master of, 30.
   Patrick, Bishop of Aberdeen, 110.
   Patrick, of Corse, 32.
   Philip, of Thornton, 67.
   Robert, 33.
   Robert, of Ludquharn, 67, 68.
   Robert, of Newtoun, 64-66.
   Sir Arthur, 110.
   Sir John, of Craigievar, 69.
   Sir Thomas, of Waterton, 59, 62.
   Sir William, of Craigievar, 61, 110.
   Thomas, of Thornton, 67.
   William, of Corse, 36.
   William, of Ludquharn, 67, 68.
   William, of Tolquhore, 4.
Ford, Elizabeth, 90.
Fordun, lands of, 34, 53.
Fotheringham, John, 13.
Fraser, Alexander, of Philorth, 4, 101.
   Andrew, of Muckalls, 4.
   John, in Elrick, 5.
   Sir Peter, of Dores, 107, 108.
   Thomas, of Strachan, 4.
   William, Chancellor of Scotland, 107.
Frazer, Margaret, 2, 107, 108.
   Sir Alexander, of Cowie, 2, 107.
   Sir John, of Strachan, 2, 107.
Fullertons, the, of Thornton, 68.

Garden, Francis, of Troup, 68.
Gardenstone, Lord, 68.
Gardin, Alexander, of Freak, 16.
   James, of Beth, 16.
   Janet, 53.
Garrioch, Mariota de, 111, 112.
Gaw, John, 35.
"Genealogie of the Strachans," 106.
Glasleter, John de, of that ilk, 9, 10.
Glegg, Rev. John, 99.
Glencairn, William, Earl of, 51, 52.
Glenkenety, lands of, 3.
   Strachans of, 3-5, 37, 48.
Godfreystown, lands of, 25.
Goislie, lands of, 50.
   Strachans, 41, 44, 50, 51, 109.
Gordon, Alexander, Earl of Sutherland, 39.
   George, Earl of Huntly, 28, 32.

Gordon—*continued*.
   George, of Newton, 62.
   James, of Newton, 62.
   John, 35.
   Lord George, 72.
   Margaret, 5.
   Sir Alexander, of Cluny, 4.
   Sir Robert, of Letterfourie, 39.
   Sir William, of Gordonstown, 111.
Gowan, Alexander, of Lismore, 34.
Gowrie, Earl of, 109.
Graham, Henry, of Morphie, 29, 109.
   Robert, of Fernyflat, 54.
   Sir Robert, of Morphie, 39.
Granard, Earl of, 110.
Grant, Rev. Ludovic, 63, 68.
Gray, Patrick, Lord, 15.
Greendew, lands of, 50.
Gregory, Captain, R.N., 92.
Grey, Elizabeth, 91.
   Lieut.-Colonel John, 91.
Guthrie, lands of, 14.
   Marion, 42.
   Sir John, 17.

HADDOW, lands of, 31.
Hamilton, James, Earl of Arran, 28, 32.
Harland, Sir Robert, 92.
Haughead, lands of, 33, 39, 45, 48, 64.
Haughhead, Strachans of, 63.
Hay, Anna, 101, 102.
   Chancellor, 44, 110.
   Elizabeth, 106.
   James, of Seggieden, 101.
   John, of Enzie, 26.
   John, of Tullibody, 108.
   Lord, 106.
   Lord Dalgettie, 106, 109.
   Margaret, 25, 27, 29, 106, 108, 109.
   Marion, 108, 109.
   William, Earl of Errol, 27, 109.
   William, of Ury, 73, 74.
Henderson, Andrew, 98.
   Bailie John, 23.
   Barbara, 88.
   Euphane, 98.
   Grizel, 100, 101.
   Margaret, 86.
   Mary, 96.
   Thomas, of Barry, 100.
   Walter, 98.
Henryson, Laurence, 40, 45, 50

Henryson—*continued*.
   Manse, 41.
   Rebecca, 41.
Hertford, Charles, Marquis of, 95.
Hillbank, Wise of, 101, 104, 105.
Home, Sir George, of Spot, 49.
Hopetoun, Lord, 72.
Hoy, Anna, 86.
Hunter, David, of Blackness, 83.
   Elizabeth, 83.
Huntersett, lands of, 30.

INCHGRAY, Strachans in, 47.
Inchtuthill, lands of, 56, 60.
   Strachans of, 59, 60, 91-95.
Inglistoun, lands of, 11, 24, 49.
Innerithnie, Strachans of, 6.
Innes, Alexander, 45.
Innoquhuly, lands of, 31, 33.
Inquest, service of, 77-80, 108.
Invercarran, battle of, 21.
Irving, Christian, 35.
   Robert, of Quhilstane, 37.

JAMES II., 3.
   III., 107.
   IV., 26, 112.
   V., 30, 53.
   VI., 19, 44, 110.
   VII., 91.
Jameson, Andrew, 75.
   Robert, 76.

KEIR, lands of, 3, 108.
Keith, Alexander, of Pitbuddlo, 96.
   Colonel John, 45.
   Elizabeth, 106.
   George, Earl Marischal, 43-45.
   Isabel, 34.
   James, of Benholme, 43-45.
   James, of Caldhame, 64.
   Margaret, 96, 97.
   Robert de, of Strathachyn, 2, 107, 108.
   Sir William, Earl Marischal of Scotland, 2, 34, 39, 45, 74, 106-108.
Kellie, barony of, 13.
Kendall, Rev. Edward, 85.
Kennedy, John, of Argeycht, 41.
   John, of Cairnmucks, 48.

Kinaldie, Strachans of, 5.
Kincairn, lands of, 18.
Kincardine, lands of, 56, 75.
Kincraigie, lands of, 32.
   Strachans of, 32.
Kinettlis, lands of, 11, 23.
   Strachans of, 23.
Kingstoun, lands of, 25.
   Strachans of, 25.
Kinnaird, lands of, 23.
Kirkbutho, lands of, 13.
Kirkheugh, lands of, 53.
Knockquharne, lands of, 32.

LANDLEYS, lands of, 25.
Lander, Sir Robert, 8, 9.
Lauriston, Mains of, 97.
Law, Alexander, 4.
Lawers, Chalmers of, 101.
Lawless, Clement, 105.
Lawson, James, of Whitesaugh, 96.
   Richard, 108.
Learmonth, James, of Balcomie, 34.
Lease of lands of Easter Guthrie, 14.
Lenturk, barony of, 30.
   Strachans of, 30, 53.
Leopold I. of Germany, 91.
Leslie, Alexander de, Earl of Ross, 2.
   General David, 21.
   John, 27-29, 99.
   Norman, 27-29.
   Sir George, of Rothes, 2.
Lesmurdie, Easter, 5.
   Strachans of, 5, 6.
Lethendie, Strachans of, 59, 88.
Letters, royal, 4, 14, 15, 44.
Lenchland, 19.
Lichtoun, Elizabeth, 27.
   Robert, of Ulyhaven, 54.
Lindesay, Alexander, of Balcarres, 41.
   David, Earl of Crawford, 3.
   David, of Balcarres, 42.
   John de, 107.
   John, of Balcarres, 41, 42.
   Margaret, 41, 42.
   Sir David, of Edzell, 41, 42.
   Sir David, of Glenesk, 41.
   Sir James de, 11.
   William de, of Byres, 3.
Lindsay, Alexander, 23, 62.
   Rev. David, 24.
   Richard, of Smythy, 23.

Livingstone, Alexander, of Dunipace, 109, 111.
   Isabel, 106, 111.
   John, of Dunipace, 42, 44.
   Margaret, of Dunipace, 30, 31, 34, 106.
   Sir David, of Dunipace, 110, 111.
Lovelace, Elizabeth, 92.
Low, David, of Laws, 96.
   Professor David, 96.
Lunan, lands of, 23.
   Wyse of, 97-101.
Lundy, Margaret, 4.

MACDONALD, Sir Donald, of Sleat, 110, 111.
Macpherson, Rev. Allan, 102.
   William, of Blairgowrie, 102.
M'Kenzie, Margaret, 101, 103.
   Sir Kenneth, of Glenbervie, 102, 103.
Mains of Thorntoun, lands of, 45, 48, 63.
   Wyse of, 96, 97.
Maitland, Alexander, 84.
   Augustus, 84.
   Frederic, 84.
   Sir Alexander, of Cliftonhall, 84.
   William, 84.
Makpesse, John, 10.
Malcolm IV., 107.
Maurent, bond of, 13, 14, 17.
Manwell, Sir Michael, 10.
Marriage, contract of, 41-43, 62.
Mathew, Mary, 79.
Mathie, John, 87.
Maule, Christian de, 7, 10.
   Elizabeth de, 15.
   Patrick de, 15, 17, 18.
   Robert de, 14, 19.
   Sir Henry, of Panmure, 7, 10.
   Sir Thomas, of Panmure, 12, 15, 17, 19.
   Walter de, of Panmure, 8.
   William de, of Panmure, 8, 9, 11.
Maxwell, Alexander, of Tealing, 20.
   David, of Tealing, 16.
   Elizabeth, 20.
   Isabel, 16.
"Memorial, a, of Strachans of Thornton," 106-112.
Mercer, Anna, 34, 35.
   Laurence, of Meiklcour, 34.
   Robert, 35.
Middleton, General, Earl of, 21, 60, 64, 87, 109, 110, 112.
   John, of Caldhame, 109.

Middleton—*continued.*
  John, of Killhill, 36.
  John, of that ilk, 110.
  lands of, 109.
  Robert, of Caddow, 41.
Mignan, Stephen, 93.
Mill of Thorntoun, lands of, 42, 63.
Milne, Dr John, 78, 80.
Monboddo, Strachans of, 26, 34, 36, 37, 42-45, 50-58, 72-79, 82-90, 98, 106, 108, 112.
Moncur or Monquhir, lands of, 7, 10, 11, 13.
Moneyethyn, lands of, 7.
Monicubo, lands of, 107, 108.
Monrenmont, Moss of, 25.
Montgomery, General Robert, 21.
Montquharie, lands of, 16.
Montrose, Marquis of, 21, 56.
  Register of Sasines, 55, 74-76, 81, 82.
  Town Records of, 75, 76.
Mophet (Moffat), John, 46.
Mortification, deed of, 107.
Morton, Earl of, Regent, 32.
Mould, William, 42.
Moyes, Hannah, 90.
Mudie, James, 81.
Murray, Sir David, of Balvaird, 28.
Musselburgh, Strachans in, 20-23.
Mylne, Robert, 35.
Myretoun, lands of, 26, 27.
  Strachans of, 41, 92,

NEWBIGGING, lands of, 30, 36.
Newton, lands of, 61.
  William, 24.
Nicolson, Colonel, 105.
Niddrie, George, 35.
Nithsdale, Earl of, 40, 56.

OCHILTREE, John de, 11.
Ochterlony, Elizabeth, 24.
  James, of Pitlewy, 13.
  John, Bishop of Brechin, 98.
  Sir James, of that ilk, 13.
  William, 17, 78, 80.
Ogilvie, Isabel, 98, 99.
  James, Earl of Airlie, 40, 43, 111.
  James, of Airlie, 4.
  John, 98.
  Lieutenant Henry, 98.
  Margaret, Countess Keith, 43-46, 111.

Ogilvie—*continued.*
  Patrick, Lord of Deskford, 56.
  Rev. Henry, of Lunan, 98, 100.
  Rev. Thomas, 98.
  Sir Francis, of Newgrange, 48, 64.
  Sir Patrick, 56.
  Wedderburn, of Islabank, 98.
Ogston, ——, of that ilk, 29, 109.
Oliphant, Sir William, of Newtoun, 37, 43.
Oliver, Dr, 70.
Orchardton, Sir Andrew, 52.
  Sir James, 52.
  Sir John, of that ilk, 51, 52.

PAGE, Anne, 103.
Panmure, lands of, 13.
Park, Hays of, 101.
Patents royal, 14, 15, 111.
Pearl, Ada, 85.
  Alice, 85.
  Catherine, 85.
  Colonel John W., 85.
  Emily, 85.
Pearson, Alexander, 6.
Peirson, Rev. William. 86.
Petrie, William, 78, 80.
Phelan, Henrietta, 105.
  William, of Rock Abbey, 105.
Phesdo, lands of, 49, 50.
  Strachans of, 85, 109.
Pitarrow, lands of, 37.
Pitcairne, William, 102.
Pitcarne, Walter, 7.
Pitgervy, lands of, 26, 27, 42.
Pitorthy, lands of, 42.
Pittendreich, lands of, 69.
Pitman, Caroline, 93.
Prendergast, Anne, 105.
  Thomas, 105.
  Sir Jeffrey, 105.
Purcell, Captain George, R.N., 85.

QUHYTLAW (Whitlaw), Robert, of Newgrange, 16.

RAIT, Anna, 52.
  Elizabeth, 110.
  Isabel, 49, 50.
  Peter, 31.
  Sir James, of Halgreen, 52.

Rait—continued.
  William, of Balmakewan, 56.
  William, of Halgreen, 35, 110.
Ramsay, Alexander, 13.
  David, of Balmain, 55, 57, 59, 62.
  Jean, 62, 63.
  Marjory, 106.
  Mary, 57, 59, 60, 65, 67.
  Sir Gilbert, 59, 62.
  Sir James, of Balmain, 51.
  Sir James, of Benholme, 63.
  William, of Balmain, 29, 106, 109.
Records, Justiciary, quoted, 43, 44.
  Privy Seal, 44, 45.
Register, Guild, of Edinburgh, 55.
  Privy Council, 37, 38, 73, 74.
Rennie, Patrick, of Usan, 90.
  Thomas Strachan, 90.
Reuny, Henry, 96.
  James, 96.
  Jane, 96.
Richards, Amelia, 84.
  Catherine, 84.
  Elizabeth, 84.
  W. P., 84.
Riddell, James, 72.
Ritchie, James, 98.
  John, 98.
Robert I. (Bruce), 2, 95, 107.
  II., 2, 25, 108.
  III., 2, 31, 108.
Robertson, Lady Elizabeth, 32.
Robinson, Isabella, 96.
Rodney, Admiral, 93.
Rollock, Rev. Alexander, 21.
Rose, Hon. George, 97.
  Margaret, 79.
  Margaret, of Kilravock, 26, 108.
  Rev. David, 79, 97.
Ross, George, Provost of Montrose, 78, 80.
  Janet, 26, 106.
  Katherine, 70.
Rossy, Edward, of that ilk, 16.
Rothes, Countess of, 2.
Ruthven, Dame Margaret, 109.
  Walter, 23.
  William, Lord, 109.

St Andrews, James, Bishop of, 3.
  James, Commendator of, 31.
  John, Archbishop of, 19.
  Laurence, Archdeacon of, 107, 112.

St Andrews—continued.
  Walter, Bishop of, 3.
  William, Bishop of, 11.
St Clare, William de, Sheriff of Edinburgh, 107.
Saltoun, Lord, 6, 107, 108.
Sandilands, Robert, 20.
Scots, Mary, Queen of, 19, 109.
Scott, Anne, 99.
  Dr Hercules, 99.
  Dr John, 99.
  Grizel, 100.
  John, 100, 101.
  Margaret, 103.
  Rev. John, 98.
Scrimgeour, Alexander, 10.
  James, 13.
  William, 10.
Seton, Alexander, of Meldrum, 23.
  Andrew, of Perbroith, 19.
Shepherd, Arthur, 97.
  John, 18.
Sibbald, David, 110.
  Sir Robert, 110.
Skethin, or Skeichen, lands of, 14, 15.
  Strachans of, 17.
Skryne, lands of, 8, 9.
Smith, Archibald, 21.
  Thomas, 21, 22.
Society, the, of Jesus, 70, 71.
Solway, battle of, 4.
Spark, Margaret, 70.
Speid, Margaret, 76, 81.
  William, 80.
Steele, Alexander, 97.
Stephens, Miss, of Letham, 90.
Stewart, Euphane, 23.
  Matthew, Earl of Lennox, 30.
  Walter, Lord of Lorne, 17.
Strachan, John, Bishop of Brechin, 85, 89.
  John, Bishop of Toronto, 89.
  John, in Sweden, 111.
  lands of, 1, 2, 3, 112.
  Sir John, 61.

STRACHANS, THE, in Aberdeen.
  Gilbert, canon, 3, 18, 19.
  James, 19.
  William, rector, 3.

STRACHANS, THE, in Arnbarrow.
  Alexander, 35.

STRACHANS, THE, *of Balhousie.*
　James, 17.
　John, 17, 18.
　Robert, 17, 18.

STRACHANS, THE, *of Bararton.*
　David, 81.

STRACHANS, THE, *of Carmyllie.*
　Alexander de, 7-14.
　David, 12-15.
　Euphane, 7.
　Helen, 16.
　Henry, 7.
　Isabella, 7, 15, 16.
　James, 12, 14-17.
　John, 11.
　Patrick, 16.
　Thomas, 7, 14, 15.
　Ysocia, 8.

STRACHANS, THE, *of Claypotts.*
　Gilbert, 16, 20.
　John, 7, 15, 18, 20.

STRACHANS, THE, *of Cliffden.*
　Amelia, 84.
　Catherine, 84.
　James, 83,
　Jane, 84.
　Sir John, 82-84.

STRACHANS, THE, *of Culloden.*
　Alexander, 112.
　George, 6, 26.

STRACHANS, THE, *of Dillievard.*
　Euphane, 106.
　John, 106.

STRACHANS, THE, *of Dyhill.*
　Dr, 112.
　John, 112.
　Professor, 112.

STRACHANS, THE, *in Edinburgh.*
　David, 46, 47.

STRACHANS, THE, *of Fettercairn.*
　James, 41, 48, 50, 56, 59, 75.

STRACHANS, THE, *of Glenkindie.*
　Adam, 3, 37.
　Alexander, 3-5, 48.

Strachans—*continued.*
　Duncan, 4.
　Margaret, 3.
　Sir Patrick, 5.
　William, 4.

STRACHANS, THE, *of Goislie.*
　Alexander, 41, 50, 109.
　John, 44, 50, 51.

STRACHANS, THE, *of Haughhead.*
　John, 63.

STRACHANS, THE, *in Inchgray.*
　William, 47.

STRACHANS, THE, *of Inchtuthill.*
　Charlotte, 94.
　David, 59.
　Dr Patrick, 92.
　Elizabeth, 93, 95.
　James, 59, 60.
　Jervis, 95.
　John, R.N., 92.
　Lieutenant Patrick, R.N., 92, 93.
　Mary, 93, 95.
　Matilda, Countess Bertholdi, 94.
　Sarah, Princess St Antimo, 95.
　Sir Richard, 93-95.
　Sir Thomas, 91, 92.

STRACHANS, THE, *in Innerithnic.*
　Arthur, 6.
　Captain John, 6.
　Margaret, 6.
　Marion, 6.

STRACHANS, THE, *of Kinaldie.*
　Patrick, 5.

STRACHANS, THE, *of Lenturk.*
　John, 30, 53.
　Thomas, 30.

STRACHANS, THE, *of Lesmurdie.*
　Andrew, 6.
　James, 5, 6.
　Patrick, 6.

STRACHANS, THE, *of Lethendie.*
　James, 59, 88.

STRACHANS, THE, *of Mill o' Glendie.*
　Alexander, 37.

Index. 121

STRACHANS, THE, of *Monboddo*.
Alexander, 77, 108.
Andrew, 106.
Anne, 88.
Beatrice, 76-79, 86, 88.
Catherine, 75.
Charles, Deputy-Governor of Guernsey, 77-80, 88, 89.
Christian, 86, 88.
David, 54, 55, 72, 77-80, 86, 87, 89.
David, Bishop of Brechin, 76-80, 85, 86, 112.
Elizabeth, 77.
George, 78, 81, 98.
Helen, 80.
Laurence, 88.
Margaret, 81, 82, 86-89, 98.
Mary, 86-88.
James, 34, 42, 51, 58, 72, 74, 77, 81, 85, 89, 106.
James, Commissary of Brechin, 78-80, 86, 87.
James, Lieutenant, R.N., 78, 80-82, 100.
Jean, 51, 52, 75, 76, 81, 87, 88.
John, 53, 75-81, 87, 106.
Robert, 77-81.
Robert, M.D., 36, 37, 43-45, 50-55, 72-77, 85, 88.
William, 26, 51, 52.

STRACHANS, THE, in *Muirailhouse*.
William, 37.

STRACHANS, THE, of *Mureton*.
John, 41, 92.
Thomas, 92.

STRACHANS, THE, in *Musselburgh*.
Archibald, Lieut.-Colonel, 20-22.
Elizabeth, 20, 22.
Helen, 20, 22.
Isabel, 20-22.
Janet, 20, 22.
Margaret, 20, 22.
Robert, 20, 23.
William, 23.

STRACHANS, THE, of *Phesdo*.
John, 85, 109.

STRACHANS, THE, of *Skethen*.
George, 17.

STRACHANS, THE, of *Turrie*.
Alexander, 78-80, 90.
Andrew, 90.
David, 90.
Elizabeth, 90.
Henry, 90.
Isabel, 90.
James, 90.
Janet, 90.
Jean, 90.
John, 90.
Patrick, 89, 90.
Thomas Rennie, 90, 91.
Walter, 90.
William, 90.

STRACHANS, THE, of *Thornton*.
Alexander, 25-30, 32-50, 53, 54, 56, 60, 66, 67, 70, 71, 74, 75, 83, 85, 92, 106, 108-110.
Andrew, 26, 31, 55, 75.
Archibald, 110.
Arthur, 110.
Christian, 108.
David, 26, 27, 106, 108-110, 112.
Duncan, 108.
Elizabeth, 29, 32, 35, 36, 51, 110.
George, 26, 35, 36, 37, 49, 74.
Grizel, 63, 68, 87.
"Father" Alexander, 70-72.
Francis, 70, 111.
Helen, 32, 33.
Henry, 46.
Isobel, 51.
James, 25, 50, 60, 62, 63-71, 107, 108, 110, 111.
Jean, 29, 32, 35, 36, 39, 63, 64, 74, 109.
John, 26, 27, 29-39, 41-43, 45, 46, 48-50, 53, 74, 98, 106, 108-112.
Joshua, 70.
Katherine, 35, 36, 51, 110.
Magdalene, 35, 36.
Margaret, 29, 37, 51, 109, 110.
Mary, 68, 110.
Rev. James, of Keith, 69, 70, 111.
Robert, 33, 34, 36, 37, 48, 49, 53, 70-72.
Thomas, 41, 110.
William, 70, 110.

STRACHANS, THE, of *Tibbertie*.
Janet, 5.
William, 5.

K

STRACHANS, THE, *of Tullyfrusky.*
   Andrew, 6.
   William, 34.

Straiton, Margaret, of Lauriston, 26, 106, 108.
Straquhan. ⎫
Strathauchin. ⎪
Strathechyn. ⎬ *See* Strachan.
Strathethyne. ⎪
Stranchin. ⎭
Strathachin, Alexander, 6.
   Alexander, of Balmaddie, 23.
   Alexander, of Brigtown, 16, 23, 24, 33.
   Alexander, of Kinettles, 23.
   David, of Mill o' Thornton, 31.
   Duncan de, 7.
   George, 4, 5, 6.
   James, of Balmaddie, 23.
   John, of Kincraigie, 32.
   Patrick, 19.
   Patrick, of Brigtown, 24.
   Robert, of Brigtown, 24.
   Thomas, of Brigtown, 24.
   Thomas, of Cairntown, 15.
Strathcathro, Turnbulls of, 98.
Strathecan, Alexander de, 3.
   Annabel, 25.
   Christian, 25.
   Donald, of Kingstoun, 25.
   John de, 1, 10, 107.
   Ranulph de, 1, 107, 112.
   Sir James de, 6, 25.
   Waltheof de, 1, 107, 112.
Strathmore, Patrick, Earl of, 88.
Strathnairn, Lord, 97.
Straton, Alexander, of that ilk, 42.
Strivelyne, William de, 3.
Stuart, David, Duke of Rothesay, 3.
   John, Earl of Carrick, 11.
   Murdoch, 2.
   Robert, Duke of Albany, 2, 3, 11, 108

TARRIE, Strachans of, 78-80, 90, 91.
Taybank, Guthries of, 101.
Taylor, Robert, 63.
Thornton, Agneta de, 6, 25, 107.
   Archibald, 19.
   Charles, of that ilk, 19.
   Gilbert, 16.
   Gilbert, of that ilk, 24.
   John, of that ilk, 7, 15.

Thornton—*continued.*
   Strachans of, 25-51, 53-56, 60, 62-72, 74, 75, 83, 85, 87, 92, 98, 106, 108-112.
   Valeus de, 6, 7.
Tibbertie, Strachans of, 5.
Tombstone inscriptions, 62, 63, 70, 82, 83, 103.
Traffy, Joseph, 85.
Trail, Rev. Professor, 99.
Troup, Agnes, 75.
Trumbill, David, 35.
Tullimadden, lands of, 25.
Tullo, lands of, 13.
Tulloch, Alexander, of Craigneston, 35, 39, 74.
   Andrew, of Craigneston, 35.
   David, of Craigneston, 35, 39, 74.
Turnbull, Catherine, 81.
   Jean, 98.
   Peter, of Smithyhill, 98.
Tyre, Walter, 23.
   William, 23.

UCHILTRE—*see* Ochiltree.
Urquhart, Alexander, of Dunlagis, 5.

WALTERS, John, 79.
Wardroper, Andrew, 100, 103.
   Euphane, 101, 103.
   Thomas, 101, 103.
Warner, Rev. Thomas, 22.
Warrants, royal, 22, 39, 40.
Warren, Sir John Borlase, 93.
Wedderburn, James, 13.
   John, 100.
   Sir Alexander, of Blackness, 100.
Wigton, Earl of, 108.
Will, Andrew, 99.
   Peter, 99.
   Rev. James, 99.
Wills of Alexander Strachan of Brigtoun, 24.
   Bishop David Strachan, 86-88.
   James Strachan, Commissary of Brechin, 88.
   James Strachan of Fettercairn, 57-59.
   James Strachan of Monboddo, 54, 55.
   Sir Alexander Strachan of Thornton, 2d Bart., 46, 47.

Index

Wise, Adam, 96.
　Alexander, 105.
　Alexander, in Montrose, 98.
　Alexander, of Lunan, 81, 97-101.
　Alexander, of Mains of Thornton, 96
　Allan, 105.
　Anna, 99, 104, 105.
　Barbara, 104.
　David, 96, 97, 99-101, 104.
　Elizabeth, 96, 98, 101.
　Emilius, 105.
　Frederick, 105.
　Grace, 101.
　Helen, 96, 99.
　Henrietta, 105.
　Henry, 99, 105.
　Isabella, 96, 97.
　James, 99, 101, 105.
　Jean, 96, 99.
　Johanna, 101.
　John, 99.
　John, of Hillsden, 95.
　John, Prior of Pluscardine, 95.
　Katherine, 99, 101.
　Margaret, 96, 98, 99, 101.
　Mary, 96, 97, 99.
　Oliver, 95.

Wise—*continued*.
　Patrick, 104.
　Rachel, 101.
　Thomas, M.D., 104, 105.
　Thomas, of Hillbank, 101, 102, 104, 105.
　William, 101, 104, 105.
Wishart, Captain Alexander, of Phesdo, 36, 38.
　Elizabeth, 77.
　James, 76.
　John, of Pitarrow, 53.
　Rev. William, 77.
Wismanstoun, lands of, 26, 27.
Wood, Andrew, of Balgeno, 88.
　John, of Craignestoan, 50.
　Margaret, 50, 51, 63, 79.
　of Balbegno, 29.
Woodfield, lands of, 2.
Wright, John, 99.
Wyse—*see* Wise.

Young, John, 6.
　John, of Lauriston, 49.

Zichny-Terraris, Emmanuel, Count of, 95.

M'Farlane & Erskine, Printers, Edinburgh.

www.ingramcontent.com/pod-product-compliance
Lightning Source LLC
Chambersburg PA
CBHW021940160426
43195CB00011B/1163